BUILD YOUR *Social* CAPITAL

A WOMAN'S GUIDE TO BUILDING A BUSINESS THAT THRIVES ON TRUST AND HUMAN CONNECTION

A fun and natural way to build a business through the power of ROR: Return on Relationships

KATRINA WAGNER

Build Your Social Capital
A Woman's Guide to Building a Business That Thrives on Trust and Human Connection

Katrina Wagner
Holly Springs, NC 27540
www.TheSocialCapitalAcademy.com

For permission requests, speaking inquiries, and bulk order purchase options, email Katrina@TheSocialCapitalAcademy.com

ISBN: 979-8-9915257-9-4

Book Design by Transcendent Publishing
Front Cover Photo by Suzel Roth, El Documentary Photographer
Back Cover Photo by Suzel Roth, El Documentary Photographer
Editing by Shelby Rawson

Printed in the United States of America

DEDICATION

*T*his book is dedicated to fearless women who manage the chaos of everyday living and bring balance and harmony to your families—women who make your house a home and raise children with dedication and love, all while putting your dreams aside to be present for your children. When the time presents itself for you to take action and turn your ideas into a business, I want you to know you're not alone. You are uniquely positioned to do things better than anyone, and when you share what you know, you make a positive impact on the world.

TABLE OF CONTENTS

Introduction vii

Chapter 1: Building Your Social Capital 1

Chapter 2: Go to School. Get a Good Job. Save Money 17

Chapter 3: The Fundamentals 23

Chapter 4: Return on Relationships .27

Chapter 5: Planting Seeds. 39

Chapter 6: Be Careful with Whom You Share Important
            Information. 45

Chapter 7: Productivity During Your Season of Growth 49

Chapter 8: Technical Skills vs. Survival Skills 57

Chapter 9: Reinventing the Wheel 63

Chapter 10: It's GO Time! 73

Chapter 11: Mitigate Risk and Financial Worry 85

Chapter 12: Your Social Capital Begins with You 97

Chapter 13: Metrics and Mastery. 115

Chapter 14: Worrier or Warrior 125

Gratitude. 131

About the Author 135

INTRODUCTION

*Y*ou're here! I am so honored that this book has found its way to you. If you're reading this, something tells me that you're ready to make a change in your life. Change can be both exhilarating and scary.

If you're like me, you're the head household coordinator. Activities director. On call for medical emergencies, planner of all schedules, and carpool attendant. Squeezed in between, you manage to fill your day with appointments, work, grocery shopping, and chaos managing, and you're always there for your friends when they need a boost of confidence. You have a dream life, but maybe something within you tells you there's more of you to explore.

Deciding to start your own business puts you in a position to create something out of nothing. It requires your attention, creative energy, and best decision-making skills. The number of things that need to be done can seem daunting. Don't let anything hold you back.

If there's a dream in your heart and you have the passion to bring it out, friend, I'm here to help you!

My first business started when I graduated college. The second business I started with my husband, and we launched fourteen days after we were married! When we picked up everything and moved across country in October 2019, I decided it was time for me to launch a new business of my own. In a place I just moved to, knowing zero people, I built a business and was able to sell that business just four years later. That brings me to you, today. I was "retired" for about thirty-two minutes before I began envisioning what my next step was going to be.

After turning forty, some things changed within me. (Can I get an "Amen" for my ladies who understand?!) I no longer want to do things that I don't like. I no longer want to spend time with people who gossip and bring out the worst in others. I want to be choosier. I want to choose where I spend my time and with whom. I want to prioritize traveling with my family and taking my daughter on as many adventures as possible. I want to instill in her a desire to go out, explore, and soak in the world around her.

At a lunch with friends, one of them asked me what I was going to do next. I said I was exploring all my options, and she said to me, "You should help women in business grow their network. No one knows how to do that better than you!" As I thought about her words, I realized she was right. Thanks, Amy!

We all have a skill that we can do unlike anyone else. I have always called the act of building my network "building my social capital." That idea grew into several different courses, programs, and an outlet for me to meet, encourage, train, and teach people how to build their own social capital.

Imagine we are sitting across the table from one another in a super-cool local coffee shop. Here are a few things I want you to know as you begin this book.

- Guess what? You've got a one-of-a-kind gift that's totally, uniquely YOU!

- No one out there can rock it like you do, in your own special way and fabulous style!

- Competition? Bring it on! You don't need to be a clone. Embrace your exceptionality!

- Hang out with positive vibes only! Cultivate a creative, open-minded approach to challenges and always be ready to explore new paths.

- Ready, set, GO! Take action NOW! Overthinking invites doubt and fear, so kickstart your dreams with bold moves!

A friend of mine had been a teacher, and everyone loved her. She loved teaching and was very good at it. When she decided to leave that profession and start her own business, all the love that people felt for her turned into confusion and worry. Instead of embracing her and thanking her for what she had done for the school, her coworkers told her, "Why would you give up? You're making a mistake." Friends of hers said, "You're really good at teaching. Why would you just give up?"

Ugh!

Those words cut, don't they?

When you take a risk, people around you try to stop you, cause you to pause, or bring doubt into the equation because they don't want to see you fail. They do, underneath the skepticism, want the best for you. They're also comfortable with you where you are now. Changing your course will change who you are, and it may cause a shift in your relationship.

As you start your business, keep this in mind:

~ *Don't take criticism from someone you wouldn't take advice from.*

~ *Everyone will have a horror story about someone's second cousin's brother who started a business and lost everything.*

~ *You will never be criticized by someone who is doing more than you. You will only be criticized by someone doing less.*

This book is a culmination of the past eighteen years of being in business for myself.

The theme you'll see is that regardless of industry or profession, the network of people in your life has an impact on how well your business grows. The people you meet have the potential to lead you to a new, ideal client, an industry leader who needs what you offer, or they can introduce you to the main decision maker for a distribution channel you could only dream about.

Everyone you meet has the ability to bring you into their sphere of influence. (That's just a fancy word for saying the people they know.)

If we go at this business-building alone, we must work tirelessly to turn every stone over. Building a network of people surrounding you requires social capital. There are certain behaviors you can choose that will make you a magnet for others to *want* to be near you.

The more people want to be near you, they come to adore you. If they understand your goals and needs, people, I have found, *do want to help you.* They just need to know how.

I am grateful for the time we will spend together here, discovering how you can build your social capital. We will laugh and share stories of things that went well and a few that didn't. We will learn together. Then, the most important part is, you take the insights you need to act as fuel for you to go and start your business.

The world needs you to be your best version of yourself.

Give us all you've got!! I'm here, and ready to cheer you on.

Chapter 1

BUILDING YOUR SOCIAL CAPITAL

Think of Social Capital as your golden ticket to building visibility and trust within your community. It's the magic sauce that makes people say, "Oh, I know her! She's awesome!" every time they see you show up, whether it's in person or online.

It's the driving force behind what would make people who spot you in a large, crowded arena get out of their seats and come find you and see you.

There's no "it factor" or "secret." It's about becoming the best version of you so that you can attract the people who can change your life and your business in ways you can't begin to dream.

Why Social Capital Matters

Building a business isn't just about having a killer product or service. It's about creating a network of relationships where people know, like, and trust you. Social Capital is the foundation that helps you achieve credibility and, ultimately, profitability. When people see you consistently showing up, delivering value, and being yourself, they start to expect great things from you. And guess what? They'll keep coming back for more!

How to Build Your Social Capital

- **Show Up Consistently:** Be there for your audience, rain or shine. Post regularly on social media, attend local events, and engage with your community in person as much as possible. Consistency builds familiarity and trust.

- **Over-Deliver Value:** Share your knowledge, offer tips, and provide solutions. When you help others succeed, they'll see you as a valuable resource and a trusted ally.

- **Be Authentic:** People can spot a fake from a mile away. Be genuine, be you. Share your journey, your successes, and yes, even your failures. Authenticity breeds connection.

- **Network Like a Pro:** Don't just build connections; build relationships. Engage in meaningful conversations, support others, and be a connector.

- **Engage and Interact:** Respond to comments, participate in discussions, and show your appreciation. Engagement creates a community of loyal supporters who will champion your brand.

By building your Social Capital, you're not just creating a network, you're creating a community that believes in you and your business. This trust translates into credibility, which leads to opportunities and, yes, profitability.

I'm peeling back my own playbook and will unleash the steps I have tested and find to work best in building your community.

Moving to Raleigh, North Carolina at the end of 2019 gave me the perfect opportunity to practice *meeting new people*. We moved across the country to a place where we didn't know even one person. We moved with the hope of building a better life for ourselves, so we didn't even have a workplace to rely on for meeting new people.

Add in the pandemic, and I had the worst-case scenario of meeting new people, establishing relationships, and building a business. But if you're looking for a sob story or a story of failure, this is not it. In every situation, there is always another way.

Built of Tough Stuff

After moving to Raleigh, North Carolina from Michigan, I decided to sign with a franchise in the insurance industry. A franchise seemed so simple. They had a proven and tested system. Their procedures were tried and true. With my background in the industry already, I thought I was making the best decision possible.

As it turned out, their systems were time-tested and true for normal operating conditions.

Cue: the world had shut down.

I officially opened May 1, 2020, and my franchise fee kicked in immediately. That meant whether or not I grew my business, the franchise fee had to be paid. Talk about pressure.

Instead of going at it the "in-person way" because that option was not available to me at that time, I got to work meeting people through two main avenues:

1. Online and organically

2. Being referred to a prospect by someone I met (personally or online)

I would do searches on social media for "Realtors in Raleigh, North Carolina." Of the thousands that popped up, I would go through and see if there were any similarities or common ground based on interests or lifestyle.

Do you know how many times I slid into people's DM's? *A lot.*

Some had a casual response: "Thanks for reaching out. I'll keep you in mind."

Some, no response at all.

The point is that showing up one time is never enough. And you don't want to be creepy either. There's a delicate cadence to this dance. Getting a response in the messages meant that they'd be able to see my profile, and I intended to give them the best of me.

It became clear that the more realtors I met in person and we got to know, the easier it would be for them to introduce me to their friends.

You Can't Be All Things to All People

Rather than focusing on everyone in the Raleigh, North Carolina area, I focused on five. Those top five had my full participation and support in whatever life was throwing our way. They would find my responses on all posts, acting as if we were already friends. In time, we became friends.

If they were hosting an Open House on a property they were listing, I'd go and stop in. Finding ways to support and bring light to what they were doing is one way you can go from not knowing people to being known by them.

Realizing that time was precious, you see now why I couldn't do this for *everyone*. Meanwhile, I still had to make sales. The old-fashioned way of sales was hard, not fun, and took a lot of time. As my awareness of people grew, I found my efforts changing as well. Focus your time and attention on people you'd like to help see grow and succeed. Be authentic and genuinely interested in their life and business. By creating a relationship based on helping someone else, they will commonly become interested in seeing you excel, too.

Take Notes

As you meet new people, you'll be tempted to remember details on your own. Don't risk it! Write it down. Take notes using whichever approach you'd like. For me, I find the simplest approach is to take notes under their contact information on your phone.

These are my **best practices** for building your own network:

- Name, business name, birthdate (if mentioned), children's names
- Spouse's name and profession

- Favorite sports teams
- Favorite brands
- Special details

Here's what it would look like on their contact card held on my iPhone under notes:

- Kara: DOB March 13; 2 kids Jimmy (age 8) and Meghan (age 5)
- Husband: Mark - chiropractor
- BIG Eagles football fans
- Loves Lilly Pulitzer
- Going to Italy this summer
- Loves dark chocolate

If you ever see them fill out a profile of *"This or That"* or *"My Favorite Things"* take note and jot down anything that's helpful.

When I met Dana at a mutual friend's holiday party, we talked a bit, but I didn't learn more than she was a realtor and was originally from New Orleans. We became friends online and about a month later, she filled out one of those *Favorite Things* questionnaires and posted it to her page. The four things I pulled from that questionnaire and put in her profile were:

1. Favorite Ice Cream: Häagen-Dazs Chocolate Peanut Butter
2. Favorite smell: Lavender
3. Liquor over beer
4. Wants to go to Austria

I had only met her once in person. Being that I was building my insurance business, collaborating with realtors was critical to growing my network. There came a time when she shared online that she was healing from foot surgery.

Using the information I now knew about her, guess what came to her doorstep as a care package? That's right! Her favorite Häagen-Dazs Chocolate Peanut Butter ice cream, a lavender-scented candle, and a hand-written card wishing her well as she recovered.

The impact that had on establishing our relationship was major. Over the course of the last five years, we've become great friends, she has entrusted me as her go-to insurance guru for her clients, and we've attended events together. And none of it would've happened without paying close attention to details and aiming to make the other person feel important.

A genuine heart is required here.

There is zero percent chance that any of this comes from a place of manipulation or coercion. Building your Social Capital takes intentional activity, willingness to play a long game, and a true desire to build relationships with others.

Dana and I just happened to be at lunch together with another woman on our power team. During lunch, we talked about plans to travel over the summer, and one of us asked where we would go if we could go anywhere.

As it was her turn to answer, she said she didn't have any idea where she'd go. Do you remember what was on the list in her contact info that I saved? We'd never talked about it before ... *ever!* So, I said something to the effect of, "Haven't you always wanted to go to Austria?"

Her eyes got so big!

We had literally never spoken about this.

She said to me with a huge smile on her face, "I don't know how you do it!"

I had done the work years ago to prepare for that one moment when I reminded her of her deep desire to explore a beautiful country. It bonded us yet again.

Then she demanded to know how I know all of this, and I told her what I've told you. Recognize little details and take notes. Keep them close, and when it's the right time, shower that person with the recognition of who they are. From experience, I will tell you these are some of my favorite moments. Remembering a small detail that they have shared with me means a great deal to both of us.

This is how relationships are formed.

Showing Gratitude

The Golden Rule is a great place to begin.

> *Treat people the way you want to be treated.*

An even better approach to building relationships with others requires the Platinum Rule.

> *Treat people the way they want to be treated.*

We could spend an entire chapter on this alone. Suffice it to say, it doesn't matter what you like, what things you like to receive or do ... doing what *you* like will never make an impact on someone else.

Focusing on what their interests are and how they like to be treated will always lead you to the point of having a tremendous impact on how they see you. Social Capital can be lost if you spend all your time trying to get people to like you.

If you've never read *The Five Love Languages* by Gary Chapman, read that next! Knowing how other people like to be shown gratitude is a game changer.

For example, if words of affirmation are important to them, then you must develop an enlightened approach to the art of handwriting thank you cards.

Here is an outline of a masterfully written thank-you card:

- Greeting
- Reflect
  - Where / when you saw them, and how that made you feel
- Specify
  - Specifically state the attributes or actions they possess that bring delight to your life or made an impact
- Support
  - One line of genuine compliment
- Salutation
- Signature

It may look like this:

Dear Britney,

It was remarkable of you to host a meet and greet at your home last Tuesday morning. It made me feel so supported to know you were willing to introduce me to your colleagues.

The fact that you hand selected the realtors who you could see being a great partner for me means a great deal. Everyone was so energetic, and it was clear they all respect you deeply.

Thank you for showing me what a true friend and partner you are!

Gratefully,

Katrina

It could also look like this:

Dear Jocelyn,

Knowing that you came all the way from out of town to our event made us all feel so important.

You must have rescheduled and moved several appointments in order to come. That is no small task, and I realize the effort you put in to attending. Everyone loved seeing you.

When you have an event that I can support you in, consider me there.

Forever thankful for your kindness,

Katrina

Gratitude can be shown in many ways. One of my favorite ways of showing gratitude is having one-of-a-kind items made that would be special to the recipient. Giving gifts that align with their hobbies or areas of interest, the impact can be so great as you start establishing a new connection. Be mindful to focus on the small details. Those details mean a great deal to the person you're trying to show appreciation to.

A friend of mine who also was a referral partner shared with me how her husband bought a new mega popcorn machine. She told me how they'd choose a movie to watch, and how much joy her husband got from popping his own popcorn. The next time I saw her, they had their very own popcorn bowls—black bowls with each of their names written on a smaller bowl and one larger bowl with their last name on it. To this day, she still sends me pictures of their movie night and popcorn bowls.

This is the kind of stuff that really makes my heart happy.

Gift giving is an art.

When your business starts getting business referred to you, your overall marketing costs go down because the cost of referrals is practically zero. That's why I put my marketing dollars into relationship building.

For my insurance agency, I focused on serving couples moving from out of state to North Carolina who needed insurance to close on their home. My entire focus was meeting and establishing relationships with realtors and mortgage lenders. I did not advertise towards the actual end client—the home buyer. I focused on building my business truly by referral.

One mortgage company I was working with resulted in over 60 percent of my new business. For a while, they were my best and most consistent referral source. A realtor may close an average of fifteen homes per year, whereas a mortgage lender may work with twenty or more new home buyers every month! Therefore, my hope was to show them how much I appreciated their partnership.

I sent cards and small thank-you gifts. During their birthday week, I would invite them to lunch or dinner. But surprisingly, they never wanted to meet for lunch or dinner. It took me a while to figure this out. After coming to understand them better, they wanted to be sure I could handle the business they sent my way and do so with absolute integrity. They valued responsiveness over gifts.

So, when the time presented itself, and they asked if I would sponsor a luncheon, they were hosting for the realtors they worked with, I realized that was the way I could show up for them. So, I happily sponsored their luncheons.

It was during one of these luncheons that I noticed they didn't have a scannable tabletop QR Code piece with their social media pages and website on it. What a useful item that would be! Working with their office manager (who became a great friend of mine as well), I told her at the start to "create it to look exactly the way you want it to look and have whatever QR codes you think are needed. Cost is no issue! This is my gift to you."

She was shocked by my willingness to gift them something of great impact for their business. She designed exactly what they would need and made it exactly the way they would want it.

When it was delivered, she called and screamed with elation! It was perfect.

Showing gratitude doesn't always have to be dollars spent.

A referral partner of mine, Britney (who also became a great friend), wrote a book about our little town of Holly Springs, North Carolina. She had interviewed the local business owners and written a beautiful article about their stories and what led them to open their shop, brewery, or restaurant in town. They had gorgeous photoshoots, and the result was a coffee table book that was from her heart to our town.

We'd just sort of met at that time. I found her to be so passionate and a firecracker and rockstar all in one. She told me about her book, and I asked her if she planned on having a book release party. She was thinking of having a small gathering to launch her book. I threw out a few questions, and by the time we were done talking, we'd decided she needed to have a major book release party!

I offered to help her in whatever way she needed to make this launch party happen. Looking back, planning her book launch party laid the real foundation of our friendship. Sharing ideas and building off of each other took this simple idea and turned it into a fantastic reflection of her heart's work and the intention of her book—to bring people together.

It didn't cost me one penny.

The benefit of supporting her in accomplishing a dream of hers resulted in a strong friendship and collaboration. I rely on her to keep me in check and help me level up any ideas I may be thinking. Working together, we can all do more.

Our goal in creating social capital is to gain the type of partnership, trust, and friendship I found in Britney.

As an aside, to show just how incredible your relationships can be when you build your business this way, here's a fun spin-off story.

Britney, a recognized member of the Triangle Real Producers and a top realtor in the Raleigh, North Carolina market, referred me to every buyer of hers. One was a couple who had moved from Colorado to Greenville, North Carolina and was relocating to Holly Springs. Talking with them, I could tell we had potential to be friends.

Fast forward. They buy their home from Britney. I become their insurance agent. And we all become friends. We celebrate 80s Dance Party Birthdays together, watch each other's kids play baseball, and then comes the biggest surprise of them all ...

Six weeks before my fortieth birthday, the three of us are all at lunch together. They pull out a box and say we are celebrating my birthday early! As the box is being unwrapped, they are staring at me with wide eyes. Britney has her camera pointed at me, videotaping every move I make.

I pull out a piece of paper that says, "Katrina's 40th Birthday Cruise to the Bahamas!" I screamed. I smiled. Then I cried. Britney has it all on tape.

Can you imagine? My two closest friends—people I hadn't met prior to 2020—were now helping me celebrate in such a huge and monumental way. Britney was a referral partner. Her buyer hired me to be their insurance agent. *Is this even real life?*

Yes, my friend, it is. This is just one story of how the relationships you build while building your business can be the launching point for an exceptional life.

When I talk about building your business in a way that strengthens your social capital, I'm really aiming to teach you how to open yourself up to be the best version of you. In turn, you can attract the people who have the potential to change both your life and your business in ways you can't begin to dream of.

This is the power of building a community. Starting your business is going to change a lot of people's lives. But it may surprise you to know it will change your life the most.

My fortieth birthday cruise with two people I would have never met had it not been for opening my business and aiming to build my network with amazing women.

SOCIAL CAPITAL HIGHLIGHTS

- **Show Up Consistently and Authentically:** Be present regularly—whether posting on social media, attending events, or engaging in person. Show your true self, including both successes and challenges, as authenticity and consistency build trust and connection.

- **Deliver Exceptional Value:** Share your expertise freely. Offer tips, provide solutions, and help others succeed. Being generous with your knowledge positions you as a trusted and valuable resource.

- **Network with Purpose:** Build relationships that matter by engaging in meaningful conversations, supporting others, and acting as a connector. Choose wisely where you invest your attention and energy—focus on connections that align with your goals.

- **Engage and Interact with Your Community:** Respond to comments, participate in discussions, and show appreciation for others. Active engagement fosters loyalty and creates a community of supporters around your brand.

- **Show Gratitude and Recognition:** Acknowledge and thank those who support you, make introductions, or offer help. Small acts of gratitude strengthen relationships and reinforce a culture of mutual respect.

Chapter 2

GO TO SCHOOL. GET A GOOD JOB. SAVE MONEY.

Leading up to college graduation, my friends were interviewing all over the country for exciting jobs in advertising, marketing, and sales. My friends who were accounting majors were hired first. They knew where they were going.

Looking back at that time, I had in my mind a three-step process to life:

1. Go to school.
2. Get a good job.
3. Save money.

It worked for generations before me, so what was my problem?

During college, I worked three jobs. I did at-home care for an elderly woman who became so close to me, she was more like family. Later, I'll share with you the importance of relationships and how it is through relationships that we really find the golden stars of life.

My other two jobs were working for the student services department at my university. Part of that included reaching out to alumni to invite them to share and continue the advancement of our free enterprise education with current students through donations or scholarship sponsorships. This role also allowed me to share what the university had to offer with prospective students. We had large-scale visitor days and during those days, I'd lead different groups on a campus tour.

This part of the job really allowed me to share my perspective. Sure, there were plenty of required parts—the buildings and historically relevant parts. On campus, there is an amazing bronze sculpture called *Lincoln on the Prairie*. It's a fourteen-foot, bronze sculpture. It depicts Abraham Lincoln riding horseback (before he became President of the United States). It's the only equestrian statue of Abraham Lincoln ever sculpted.

Working this job allowed me the chance to practice the art of selling. Every family that came to visit the campus was essentially interviewing us (a collective us). They needed to determine if it was a good fit for their child. Likewise, each prospective student was making a major decision usually based on a four-hour visit to campus.

I took this role super seriously. I learned over time that it wasn't so much whether we were a good fit for each other at that time, but rather, if this campus and school could help mold that young person into the future business leader they wanted to become. If that connection was made, then it would be a match made in business heaven.

The third job was offered to me after one random opportunity.

Oprah Winfrey says, "Luck happens when preparation meets opportunity."

I agree with her. My luck showed up the day the leader of the campus visit was running late ... I mean, really late.

Some of the advisors were talking about switching the schedule around because they didn't have a keynote speaker to address the entire audience visiting campus. There were a few hundred people in an auditorium waiting to hear from a prestigious university leader.

I knew I could do it.

When I offered to speak in the prestigious leader's absence, some looked at me with a face that read: "We've never had a student speak before."

Fortunately, I went to an incredible university. A university that practiced everything they taught us. With the eagerness of others to speak publicly being normally *low* ... I said, "You know me. You can trust me. I won't let you down." They trusted me because I had already deposited into my social capital account with them. My reputation was strong, and they had faith that I could deliver.

They introduced me ... Fortunately, I was a very active student, and at least held the official title of Student Body President and served as the President of the Student Senate, so in that way, I was a young, prestigious university leader.

You want to know what?

It went awesomely! I spoke for about fifteen minutes. My time on stage centered around campus engagement, our professors, and student life. It wasn't hard because I shared real life experiences and stories about what it was like as a student. It was engaging and fun, and the feedback was super positive.

Unexpectedly, I had secured a permanent place on the schedule! And they paid me for the time I spoke, too.

This was a major "aha moment" for me in life. If you have abilities and knowledge, you can be paid for what you know. People appreciate your ideas and opinions. The major takeaway: you can be paid for your organized thoughts.

Two impactful opportunities occurred during my role as a speaker at these events.

1. The owner of a nearby Dale Carnegie Training® was attending the Visitors Day with his daughter. We ran into one another later that day in the cafeteria, and he complimented me, then offered to sponsor me and a friend of mine through *The Sales Advantage*. We quickly accepted, and after graduation, we took that course every week for six weeks … The class was two hours away and started at 6:00 p.m. We didn't care. We were young, and time didn't affect us. What an opportunity that impacted my entire life!

2. While giving a guided campus tour, unbeknownst to me, an Executive Vice President of the Estee Lauder Corporation was attending that day with her daughter. We got to talking, and by the end of the campus tour, she passed me her card and said that if I ever wanted to work for them, give her a direct call. I called and she wasn't bluffing. I started working in August.

It turns out that my entrepreneurial spirit was lit sometime in my youth. It could have been the lawn mowing. (I was known for diagonal mowing.) My dad taught me to keep the lines straight!

It could have been after turning sixteen. I used my ability to play the piano, and like my mom, became a music minister at church. I had a skill (piano playing), and I taught myself how to play the pipe organ and sing at the same time. Then, I developed additional skills to lead a choir of adults and eventually taught a children's choir how to sing, praise, and worship. This is the one skill that I have always been able to lean on.

Skills = Options. Instead of trading time for money, if you have skills and knowledge that other people seek, you can be paid for those various abilities.

So, I learned that going to school, getting a good job, and saving money wasn't the plan for me.

Rather, it was:

1. Develop desirable skills.
2. Start a business.
3. Leverage those skills to help others achieve their goals.

Looking back over the last eighteen years, I have:

- Started a consulting company in Metro-Detroit focused on internal operations consulting.
- Joined efforts with my husband and two weeks after we were married, opened his insurance agency which still is ongoing.

- Moved to Raleigh, North Carolina and opened my own insurance agency in May 2020. Knowing zero people upon moving, I built that company up to sell profitably in May 2024.

This brings us to now. With eighteen years of entrepreneurial experience and having felt every blunt reality of being in business for myself, I am eager to help you build the business you've wanted to build.

Launching is easy. Staying the course is hard.

This book is a passion project from me to women with vision and voice.

So now that you know me, I promise to ride this tidal wave of business ownership with you. There will be major high points. There will be lows that cause you to question if this is the right move. Whatever is right for you, I've got you, friend.

If it's a business you want to start, then I'm here to help make it practical.

If there are certain pain points you're trying to solve—don't wait—skip to that section. Use this book to guide you and empower you, serving as a reminder that you're not in this alone.

SOCIAL CAPITAL HIGHLIGHTS

- Just because everyone else is doing it one way, doesn't mean your way can't work.
- Develop desirable skills.
- Launching is easy. Staying the course is hard.

Chapter 3

THE FUNDAMENTALS

*U*sing your own, unique special skills, visualize what you can do better than anyone. Everyone has their own way of creating something, so don't waste a single minute on comparing yourself to anyone else. You see, friend, if there is a need for what you do, your ideal customer is waiting to find you!

Competition is healthy.

Options are awesome.

You don't have to be like that guy you see online who is in the same general field as you. You're not seeking the same clients. If your style is different, it'll attract your ideal customer. That's the beauty of business. We can serve our people in the way they want, all while not being like the other guy.

Be you. You're bold! You're beautiful! You're perfectly you! There is no one who is like you, has your keen sense, or sees things the way you do ... Share what you have with the world.

Here are the basic fundamental steps to starting your business:

- Define Your Business

  What could you do for five hours straight and not think of as "work?" What problem can you solve? What information do you have that solves a recurring issue for a specific target market?

- Create a Business Plan

  Separate your ideas into actionable items. Which products will you offer? What prices? What advertising approaches are you looking to implement?

- File Your Articles of Organization with Your State

  Choose your business name. Decide on your structure (LLC, Corporation, S-Corp, Sole Proprietorship, etc.) There are usually both a filing fee and an annual registration fee required for all years you're in business.

- Apply for Your Employee Identification Number (EIN)

  Head to the IRS website and apply for your EIN. It's like your Social Security Number, but it's for your business. This is important for many reasons.

- Acquire Licenses, Permits (if required), and Insurance.

  Risk can follow you anywhere, which is why having a commercial business insurance policy is warranted. Your personal insurance is to protect you personally. When it comes to your operating a business and doing "business activity," your personal policies may not extend that far. Don't learn this lesson too late.

- Open a Business Banking Account

  Congratulations! When accepting money for a business, keeping it separate from your personal finances will help you avoid any future problems.

- Create a Brand Identity

  Now comes the creative part! Create your brand. Choose your brand colors and have a cool logo made. Create all marketable materials needed for you to be visible. Using its free service, Canva is a great place to start. When you make a business email address, try to avoid making it too long or too goofy. All things related to your business should be intentional and follow a verified and continuous look and feel.

- Build Your Network and Grow

  Thinking as a business owner is going to stretch your mind and cause you to think differently. Expose the areas of your mind that limit you. If you have more negative talk towards yourself, you'll find yourself consistently stuck.

Friend, building a business takes guts. It isn't for the weak. If it were easy, everyone would do it. It's not easy. It's hard, and sometimes it will seem impossible. You have within you a certain spark that is yearning to catch on fire ... Give it room to grow. You'll find that the answers are all around you.

You're not alone.

People open businesses and close them before they ever take off. *Why is that?*

You must be willing to push beyond thoughts and actions in a way that is different from everyone else. Blow past uncertainty like it's a bad disease. Don't stop in the town of desperation. Plant yourself in soil that will be sturdy enough to keep you grounded and give you room to expand.

SOCIAL CAPITAL HIGHLIGHTS

- Competition is healthy.
- Your competition is not seeking the same target market you are. Be You!
- Be willing to push beyond thoughts and actions in a way that is different from everyone else.

Chapter 4

RETURN ON RELATIONSHIPS

*I*nnovation is a skillset. It relies on creative thinking, the ability to see things from an angle most people miss. Find ways to practice being innovative. Like any muscle, it takes practice to strengthen your innovation muscle.

Remember, you're doing something that not many people attempt. Look around you and at the closest friends you have, if no one is a business owner, then you'll need to expand your circle.

You remember the phrase, "Two heads are better than one." Three heads are better than two!

When I started my first business, I was twenty-two and moved to Metro-Detroit. I was confronted with several reasons why I shouldn't open a business:

1. No guarantee I'd make a living.
2. I was too young.
3. I'd likely fail.
4. I didn't know anyone who owned a business at my age.

5. I had zero money.
6. Was I trying to be someone I wasn't?
7. Would this hurt my prospects of finding a boyfriend or future husband?
8. I didn't think my family approved of the venture.
9. The risk that I would waste all this time and have no experience to show for it.
10. No one would want what I had to offer.

Whooooof. Those are still heavy, reading them today. Those very thoughts spun through my head—some days louder than others.

Remember I said I had started working for the Estee Lauder Corporation in August? I worked there for exactly twelve months. During that time, I hustled with the extra hours I had to meet other business people and grow my network.

It hit me. People who knew me would refer me, and if they referred me to prospects, I'd overcome almost all of those worries and it'd make the sales process much more manageable. I had graduated from the sales course we spoke about in Chapter One, so I was armed with sales training. I needed to overcome the fact that I had zero network, and so I started there.

There are different ways to think about how people can help you in your business.

- **Regular New Business Acquisition**
  This is a result of pounding the pavement. You go, search, hunt, and hopefully *bring in* new accounts or clients to your business. This takes a lot of time, recurring activity and

communication, overcoming objections and pricing hurdles, and a catch-and-release approach that can be daunting.

- **Champions**

  These are the rock star people in your life who root for you and sing your praises around town! They share your posts, they LIKE your stories, and they share your content on their page just to help. They have no ulterior motives. Champions may have never bought your service or used your product. But ... they believe in YOU!!

  If you find yourself stuck in a position and you need help, reach out to your Champions. They want to help you and do help you in ways you don't even ask them to. Treasure these champions. They are important to keep close and to show gratitude towards.

- **Referrals**

  This is the skill of partnering with other professionals where there is an ease in referring business to one another. The highest cost of this is *time*. Time is required to establish trust between referral partners. The long-term benefit can be alarmingly impressive!

  When you track your business, it's most effective to follow this process:

  > **1st Tier Referral.** Tori is referred to you by your referral partner, Jackie.
  >
  > **2nd Tier Referral.** Tori refers you to her sister, Meghan.

> **3rd Tier Referral.** Meghan adores you and refers you to Claudia.
>
> **4th Tier Referral.** Claudia introduces you to Amy, who opens her entire world to you.
>
> **5th Tier Referral.** Every opportunity that crosses your way from Amy all stems back to when Jackie, your referral partner, referred you to Tori.

This is a real and powerful approach to business. I submit to you that every business has the ability to benefit from the power of referral partners.

Here is a real-life example. As an Insurance Agent, I worked closely with realtors.

Amanda, my own realtor, asked me to sponsor a luncheon for her real estate team.

> **1st Tier.** Amanda introduced me to every realtor on her team.
>
> **1st Tier.** Amanda referred me to Carmen, a mortgage lender.
>
> **2nd Tier.** Carmen invited me to host a luncheon for her realtor friends.
>
> **2nd Tier.** Carmen refers <u>all of their clients</u> to me for an insurance review.
>
> **3rd Tier.** Susan, from Carmen's luncheon, refers me to her buyers.

3rd Tier. Tammy, from Carmen's luncheon, refers me to her buyers.

3rd Tier. Justin, from Carmen's Luncheon, refers me to his buyers.

4th Tier. Carmen's clients, Judy and Mike, buy their insurance from me.

5th Tier. Mike's parents are moving to Raleigh, and he refers me to them for insurance.

I could go on and have several examples of this very thing. It was all thanks to Amanda and her first being willing to collaborate that this line of business started to blossom. The power of tracking your referrals shows you that business between people often starts from one person having a positive experience with you, and then they tell others.

Using this process of referral-based business can have a great impact on what you can accomplish. Furthermore, referrals tend to be higher-quality prospects. They have fewer buyer objections, and they tend to have longer retention.

The key is that starting a business requires building a network of people. You'll never be disappointed investing in relationships. One person's belief in you has the ability to make your business explode.

These skills aided me greatly as I met new people:

1. First Impression
2. Conversational Engagements of Three to Five Minutes

3. Longer Form Communication: Ten-Minute Overview of My Business

4. Becoming a Resource of Talent

5. Knowing How to Respond with Grace

Power of First Impressions

Meeting people is the perfect opportunity to make a great first impression. The purpose of this skill is to respond with captivating answers to those initial questions. You're getting to know one another, and in a short timeframe, deciding if there's enough motivation to carry on a full conversation. Use this time to give answers that are interesting.

Common Question: So, tell me what is it you do?

Captivating Example: You're an Interior Designer

Have you ever bought something at the store and loved it only to get home and it somehow doesn't go with anything? (I wait for a head nod because we've all done this.) I work with women who want their home to reflect their style but have a hard time achieving it. I help by teaching them how to place their furniture, area rugs, and art in their home to communicate the message they are trying to achieve.

If done correctly, you should get a response asking for more information.

Follow-up Question: How do you do this?

It's a fun process. I get to know their style and objectives for the rooms, and we go from there. (Shift energy a bit higher.) You know, I also do something called "shop your home," where I rearrange and reposition items they already own to give the space a different feel. Having a designer's eye can really help achieve the look. My clients say it's easier than they thought, and they ultimately get much more for their money.

The best scenario you'd get is one more follow-up question.

Second Follow-up Question: *How do people find you?* (This is where you teach them how to refer you.)

I'm so glad you asked! My clients are usually referred to me by their realtor. They gift them a "shop your home" session with me upon closing. So, while I work specifically with women who own a home they've just bought and can't figure out where everything should go, my actual best introduction is to realtors who love their buyer clients so much, they'd like to make sure their new house does become their home.

The Sizzler: Do you happen to know any realtors who show love to their clients at closing with gifts? I'd love to meet them.

Why would we add that sizzler in? Because if you ask someone for help, chances are they will help you! In a first impression conversation, you've just done the following:

1. Given them a memorable way to remember what you do

2. Given one or two examples of who uses your services (always focus on ideal client examples)

3. Shared how you get introduced to your new clients (your preferable approach)

4. Asked for a personal introduction to your ideal referral partner

Networking is all about expanding your relationships.

*Pro Tip: If that person does know a realtor and that person is at the event that night, say, "Would you mind introducing me to them?"

When you meet that person: Be curious about that realtor (NOT talking about yourself).

Ask them: Where does most of your business get transacted?

- If they say forty miles away from you and that is not an ideal partner for you in doing your work, you know you can keep the conversation short. Feel free to share what you do, but thank them and continue seeking an ideal partner.

- If you find them to be a potentially good fit with your work, ask them questions about how they show their buyers appreciation after the sale. In a supportive way, share how you offer a gift for new families moving into their home with the "shop your home" session.

- The most ideal outcome is to have enough interest in one another to set up an in-person follow-up appointment. Something casual—coffee or a local café. Relationships take nurturing. Don't expect to close a deal. This isn't a sale. It's a way to build camaraderie and trust.

The Follow-Up:
Send a personal, handwritten thank-you card to the person who did the personal introduction. A follow-up note from me would look like this:

> *Dear Jennifer,*
>
> *It was such a pleasure meeting you at last night's Solve for a Cause event. I'm glad I got to meet you.*
>
> *Thank you for your kindness and asking about my business. It was wonderful to share with you.*
>
> *The fact that you took your time to personally introduce me to (insert name of realtor) at the event speaks volumes of your generous character. It was an extraordinary step for someone you just met.*
>
> *If your schedule allows for it, I'd like to meet you for lunch and explore how I can help you.*
>
> *Next week?*
>
> *Gratefully,*
>
> *Katrina*

This is an example of what **not** to write:

> *Jennifer –*
>
> *Thanks for the introduction to (insert realtors name). He doesn't work in my area so it won't work out. Oh, well. We tried.*
>
> *-Katrina*

Do you notice the difference? There's a world of difference between those two examples.

The best thing to do is to compliment the behavior you'd like to see more of. You spend time talking about what was good—nothing about the outcome. In this instance, if they knew one realtor, maybe they know another. At this point in the new relationship, it's your turn to completely dive into their business and their interests, and uncover how you can return the favor.

By meeting in person the next time, you have more of a time commitment with one another. Go to that lunch prepared to ask several questions to uncover similarities and common interests, and ultimately lead to the main event: *Who do they need to meet to take their business to the next level?*

If you don't know anyone that they need to know, it's okay. The question itself is powerful. Be sincere, and respond:

> *While I'm not sure I currently know anyone in that role,*
> *I do promise to see if anyone in my network might. Will*
> *you give me the next thirty days to see what I can find?*

For your business, you have a short game: Make sales now. For your long game, you'll be nurturing your relationships both online and in person. Both take time. You must show up, be present, gain visibility, and ultimately, become a leader in your area of expertise.

Relying on only one part of growth makes for an unstable future. If you focus solely on social marketing, and have zero human contact in the real world, what happens when your page gets shut down or the page gets hacked?

Whether you're a solopreneur or have a team of people working around you, you are built to be with others. For your own benefit, find a way to always interact in person with other business people. It keeps you sharp and relevant.

SOCIAL CAPITAL HIGHLIGHTS

- Innovation is a skillset that needs to be exercised.
- Referral business has fewer objections and longer retention.
- Tracking referrals is a powerful metric.
- First impression conversations are critical to practice.
- Handwritten *Thank You* cards never go out of style.

Chapter 5

PLANTING SEEDS

My most recent business was a franchise in the insurance industry. I signed the contract in March of 2020 and launched my brand-new agency on May 1ˢᵗ that year.

One thing I looked forward to with buying into a franchise was *process*. It was all decided, and the plan was clear. To think I would get to apply everything I already knew to a proven system made a lot of sense to me.

That is, until phrases like, *"Two weeks to slow the spread"* started being used every two weeks. By the time I launched in May, everything was shut down.

My husband Ryan and I moved to Raleigh, North Carolina. We had recognized that while there was happiness in our life in Michigan, we weren't loving our life. Couple that with health issues and terribly cold polar-vortex winters, and we knew that we needed to decide for ourselves how our life was going to be lived.

We made a list. Our top priorities were:

- Average year-round temperature 55 or higher
- Major sports teams (Ryan is a huge sports fan)
- Diverse economy
- A place where people were kind and happy

We would rent a house for one week at a time. We visited several cities across the country as we considered where we should move. In Summerlin, Nevada, we rented a house with a pool in the back-yard. We went back to that city twice because it was so attractive!!

Our last city on the list was Raleigh, North Carolina. We came down for a week in early February 2019. We rented a house in a neighborhood just outside of Raleigh. Amanda (whom I told you about in the last chapter) owned the home we were renting. I chose to rent her house because she was a realtor and could show us what we needed to see during our exploration trip. During our stay, she showed us many communities and gave us a good tour of how people lived.

Something very odd happened as we drove down the streets in these communities. People were waving to us as we drove by. They even had smiles on their faces! I remember standing in line at Starbucks in Morrisville, North Carolina. The gentlemen in front of me had a University of Michigan pin on his bag.

I asked if he was from Michigan and something miraculous hap-pened ... We had a delightful chit-chat. This kind of thing did not happen back at home. It was so cool and so nice to just have a simple conversation with someone, and then we went about our day.

Getting back into the car, I told my husband, "I just met someone who moved here from Michigan, and he said he loved living here!"

We went to a Carolina Hurricanes hockey game. As major Red Wings fans, being in another stadium felt like we were cheating on good ol' Hockey Town, but we needed to experience it for ourselves! We loved the atmosphere and were taken aback by how nice everyone in the stadium was.

By day five, we had found a vacant lot of land that was slated to have a gorgeous home built on it in a golf course community that checked off every hope we could think of. We paid our deposit and the rest is history.

We weren't running away from our life. We were *choosing life!* Instead of living where we were born, we chose to create a new mold. We chose what was important to us, and we took action. None of our friends did this. We were the weirdos.

Go ahead. Be weird. It's okay. In fact, it's awesome.

When we moved to North Carolina in October 2020, we didn't know a single person. No one whatsoever. We didn't move because of a job relocation. We didn't have a pressing reason other than we desired to build a life we loved.

Moving allowed me to expand my mind to what I wanted to do. My husband's office that we opened together would remain open, and it became an area of opportunity for me.

Ultimately, I chose to go the franchise route and stay in the insurance industry.

The week I opened, my beautiful downtown Raleigh office building was a part of the riots that were happening in major cities across the country. Everything I had planned and strategized for and the people I was going to meet all turned out to be for naught.

The only move I had was *to pivot.*

Rework the entire mainframe.

Redesign every approach to meeting people.

Since I knew literally zero people, I needed to go full force into building a network—both online and in person. The pandemic surely put a major damper on my fun plans. But it wasn't going to stop me.

Making lemonade out of these lemons proved to be harder and more challenging than I ever expected. But I had a franchise fee to pay and a business to build, so there was no time for tears.

My plan: *start local.*

We chose our community for many reasons, and living there during the pandemic made the experience far less stressful and frightening compared to other places. The weather was pleasant enough that we could go outside frequently and take walks, even if we had to do so alone.

Keeping six feet away, we would sometimes cross paths with people. When we engaged with them, I would pay close attention to their name, where they lived and what they did professionally. My follow up was to find them on the community Facebook page and "friend" them.

As I met more people, I paid close attention to their interests, families, and activities and how long they had lived in the area.

I have found that people want to help others.

As a newcomer and new business owner in the area, I relied heavily on my ability to survive and thrive in social interactions, no matter what kind they were. Gone were the "pop-ins" where I'd bring a fun candy jar to an office to introduce myself. Nope! Those days were long gone.

We attended every single event we were invited to.

- Driveway dinner with neighbors   Yup!
- Chili Cook Off   Yup!
- Baby shower for someone I'd never met   Yup!

We attended every event held at our clubhouse. Music bingo was my ultimate favorite! I remember how uncomfortable it was walking into a large venue without knowing a single person. I can still feel the awkward smiles as I longed for the day someone would actually know who we were.

While in line for anything, I would start a little chit-chat with the person in front of me. Those were the days of building up a reservoir of information. The more we went to events, the more faces looked familiar.

As we became familiar faces to other people, they would give a nice glance and wave from across the room. That is when the hard work started feeling like it was paying off.

The very first woman I met when we moved, Suzel, is the kind of lady who lives to bring people together. She is my photographer and the talented eye behind the lens of the images on the back of this book. She invited me to a lady's dinner with about ten other women when I had just moved in. I did not know anyone. We had the normal polite conversations and simple interactions. Those were the days when I was growing my visibility in my community.

In this stage of building my network, I focused on making simple, genuine connections. It doesn't matter how much you know or what you do; if people don't trust you or like you as a person, they won't be interested in learning about what you do or how you can help them, or even consider helping you.

SOCIAL CAPITAL HIGHLIGHTS

1. Plan for what you can.
2. Pivot when you need to.
3. Grow your network, starting with simple, genuine connections.

Chapter 6

BE CAREFUL WITH WHOM YOU SHARE IMPORTANT INFORMATION

*H*ave you ever shared something important to you with someone, only to have that person shut that idea down? I learned early on to be careful with whom you share important information.

As someone who is starting your own business, you may have learned this lesson already.

Our daughter was four the year we decided to take our life in a different direction. We were moving across the country towards something that we were choosing. However, for many around us, it only looked like *WARNING!! ABORT MISSION!! TERRIBLE DECISION AHEAD!!!*

We had been thinking about and planning this potential move for a good three years or more. And we had been talking about the idea for over five years.

When are the streetlights of life all green?

Never!

At some point you have to stop talking about it, and either do it or shut up about it.

So, at the point when Raleigh, North Carolina was our destination and we were building a new home in a place we had only visited for seven days, I'm sure to many on the outside that it looked foolish.

Whether it's moving across the country, quitting your job, or choosing to take a gamble on yourself and start your own business, many on the outside won't understand.

As the recipient of many pieces of advice, some that stick out for me are:

1. How will you make money?
2. You're ruining your life!
3. You're going to regret this.
4. Who will hire you after you've had so much time not being employed?
5. You must put in the time to get promoted.
6. Don't be so shortsighted.
7. You're not thinking straight.
8. You're being impulsive.
9. This is way too risky.
10. You have too much to lose!

The best thing I can tell you is: *People who have never done it will always try to talk you out of it.*

Want to hear the loudest naysayers? People who have had ideas and never pursued them. They've squelched their own innovations and ideas in order to have security. That's a noble thing. Security is noble. Protecting and providing for one's family is noble.

Reality tells us that there is a lot of inherent risk associated with launching your own business. The surprising thing is that usually the people who are closest to us are the ones who are loudest about not wanting us to *fail.*

Owning your own business has no guarantees. No promises. No consistency in paycheck. In fact, there may be times when you do not get paid. There may be times when you need to take on a side hustle to make ends meet. If you have employees, they and all your vendors might get paid first, and if there is nothing left at the end, you go without. (Been there and felt that.)

I can tell you firsthand that believing in yourself and working for the benefit of your family is the most intense kind of motivation. It triggers your fight or flight instinct. For many, this instinct is so strong that they give up and return to the comfort of security. There is a lot of comfort in security, and a great life can be built around it. If that's where you're meant to be, I support you, my friend.

If there's a nudge inside you that screams for freedom, how many times have you heard it only to silence it and move on to something else? What do you have to lose by giving it your best shot?

While people in your life always want to see you do well and succeed, sometimes they just don't know how to best support you.
So, as you start your business and see a few wins, be mindful
whom you share those wins with. In my own experience, sharing
ideas with the right people can help you clarify and hone your
creative energy.

Sharing is good. Choose wisely whom you share your news with
as you go out into the world.

SOCIAL CAPITAL HIGHLIGHTS

- The streetlights of life are never all green.
- People who have never done it will always try to talk you out of it.
- Choose wisely whom you share your news with.

Chapter 7

PRODUCTIVITY DURING YOUR SEASON OF GROWTH

If you're in a season of growing your business, there are a few important things you can do to ensure you're able to be productive, not just busy.

This part is practical.

❏ **Turn off all smart phone notifications. Yes ... All of them.**

The senseless tugging at your mind when you see six notifications from your favorite app won't take your time now. Don't worry, the notifications will be there when you open it again.

❏ **When working, set a timer for twenty-five minutes and do not check your phone.**

If getting started is the hard part, set the timer. Twenty-five minutes is a good amount of time to dedicate to whatever is in front of you. My first twenty-five is for my random task list. I know I can't get to the good stuff without sorting through those random family or daily items that always nag me in my mind.

My second, third, and every other twenty-five is far more productive. I get to a point that by three sets of twenty-five I'm so on fire, it's *hard to stop me!* I'm so focused and on a roll. Try it.

❏ **Unsubscribe or cancel all email subscriptions that waste your time.**

If a company is emailing you every single day about their sales promotions, the only thing to do is to realize that you're on their email distribution list. (If you don't have one for your business, let that be a hint to start yours.) But still, unsubscribe. Free your mind and your time!

❏ **Remove all notifications from your desktop computer.**

For all the reasons above, no one who is constantly getting interrupted is a high performer.

❏ **Delegate or hire out tasks that take time and energy away from your top priorities.**

In my own life, I find doing laundry the most time consuming. Who is like me? I can wash all the clothes. No trouble. It's the folding and putting them away part that can take weeks. So, we have a wonderful woman who comes every Monday at 9:00 a.m., and she folds and puts everything away. My life runs on track because of the time she gives me to focus on things that impact our family in a different way.

Whatever task it is for you, try delegating or hiring it out for a month. The time you get back and are able to invest in doing something else may be the time you needed to literally make major waves in your work!

☐ **Remember to eat. A meal plan or meal prepping allows you to stay the course during the day.**

A friend of mine told me that if she can't find something quick to eat when working from home, then it's Oreos and Diet Coke for her. How many of us are running on low energy because we aren't fueling our bodies well?

Eating is important. Planning ahead of time can save the stomachache of regret from hitting you all too often.

☐ **Implement Inbox Zero**

This idea may be new to you. When I first implemented it, I had over five thousand emails in my inbox!!! That pains me to look back on. Now, the ease of managing to-dos and follow-ups is so much easier.

This approach will help you manage your emails more efficiently by ensuring that only action-required emails remain in your inbox.

Here are the four steps to accomplish Inbox Zero:

1. **Set Up a "Completed" Folder:** Create a new folder in your email and name it "Completed." This will be the destination for all emails that do not require further action.

2. **Read Through & Manage Your Emails Regularly:** Quickly decide if an email requires action, can be archived, or needs to be deleted.

3. **Move Emails to "Completed":** For emails that have been read and do not require any further action, move them to the "Completed" folder. This helps keep your inbox clutter-free.

4. **Create Action Folders:** For emails that require action but can't be addressed immediately, create subfolders such as "Action Needed" or "Follow Up." Move these emails to the appropriate folder to ensure they are not forgotten. Regular review of this folder helps keep things moving.

Applying the Inbox Zero approach to managing my email has been a game-changer, especially when it comes to staying on top of follow-ups. By organizing my inbox and keeping it clean, I've eliminated the overwhelming clutter that has often caused important messages to slip through the cracks.

With a streamlined system in place, I can easily spot and prioritize the emails that need attention, making follow-ups seamless and efficient. This practice not only keeps my communication flowing smoothly but also frees up valuable time.

Advanced thinkers understand the importance of identifying where time is wasted and transforming those areas into assets. By applying strategies like Inbox Zero, you turn a potential time-drain into a powerful tool that works for you, letting you focus on what truly matters.

Considering the change in habit with my email inbox, these are the true benefits:

- *Enhanced Focus:* A clutter-free inbox allows you to focus on important tasks without the distraction of unnecessary emails.

- *Increased Productivity*: By organizing your emails and keeping only actionable items in your inbox, you'll spend less time searching for information and more time on meaningful work.

- *Reduced Stress*: A clean and organized inbox reduces the feeling of being overwhelmed by email, leading to lower stress levels.

- *Improved Time Management*: Efficient email management helps you to prioritize tasks better and to allocate time effectively for important activities.

- *Better Follow-Up*: With a system in place for action-required emails, you'll improve your follow-up process and ensure that important tasks are not overlooked.

Implementing Inbox Zero can significantly improve your workflow and individual productivity. The number of items I would forget about because everything was stored in my inbox became a struggle. Learn from my experience. Adopt this concept and it will make your growth in business easier to navigate.

❐ **Grocery delivery on Sunday afternoons allows you to stay on budget and be ready for the week.**

On Sunday afternoons, I have a delivery dropped off between 5:00 and 7:00 p.m. It has made Mondays, Tuesdays, and every day after that run smoother. I don't impulse buy. It's a beautiful thing.

Some people say that you have to burn the candle at both ends at the beginning. Well, everything worth doing takes work. But you don't have to give up everything to get ahead.

If you're going to be steering your own ship, you decide when and how that looks.

What times of the day are you *most creative? Most energetic?* Use these times to plan, create content, record videos for your social media, and develop new products prototypes.

When do you experience a *natural energy lull?* Use this time to back away from the creative arm of your business and go for a walk, shut the computer off, and do other tasks.

Now that you have options, create a schedule that enhances your abilities and natural rhythm. And be patient with yourself. You're building something brand new. Sure, businesses exist. But nothing like the one you're building!

Enjoy the fast-paced and often intense ride of starting a new business. If you get tired, invest in your rest so you're ready to get back at it. If I could give you a pen to design everything you want your life to have in it, what would your design look like?

If you've not dreamt about what that looks like for you, maybe it's a good exercise for tonight.

- What are the nonnegotiable parts about the life you'd like to create?
- What dreams do you wish to fulfill? What freedoms do you want?
- What experiences or life luxuries do you want your family to have?

Luxuries don't have to be luxurious. The luxury of taking Fridays off could be one. Or attending every school event your child has is a luxury.

What are the luxuries you seek? Do you want to work really, really hard from 10:00 a.m. to 3:00 p.m.? Cool. You can do that. Whatever you want, you're working towards that. Just because you don't have it today doesn't mean it's not worth working towards.

You've got this, friend. I believe in you.

SOCIAL CAPITAL HIGHLIGHTS

- Aim to be productive, not busy.
- Turn off all notifications.
- Implement Inbox Zero.
- Delegate tasks that open up your schedule.

.

Chapter 8

TECHNICAL SKILLS
VS. SURVIVAL SKILLS

I f you're reading this, you're probably knee-deep in the exhilarating, chaotic, and rewarding journey of running your own business. Whether you're in year one or closing in on year three, I'm here to give you a big, virtual high-five and some serious girl-boss vibes to keep you going strong.

Let's dive into a topic that's near and dear to all our hearts: Technical Skills vs. Survival Skills in business. Trust me, navigating this balance is like trying to ride a unicycle while juggling. But don't worry, we're about to break it down together.

Technical Skills: The Backbone of Your Expertise

Remember those endless nights studying in school, trying to master every little detail of your chosen field? Yep, those were the days we honed our technical skills. Whether you're an ace at graphic design, a coding ninja, a culinary wizard, or a financial whiz, these technical skills are what make you amazing at your job. They are the precision tools in your tool kit, allowing you to perfect your craft and shine bright in your industry.

Perfecting Your Craft

Technical skills are your bread and butter. They're what clients come to you for and what you build your reputation on. Mastery in your field is crucial because it's your calling card. When you're technically proficient, you deliver quality, and quality keeps customers coming back for more.

But here's the thing: technical skills alone aren't enough to keep your business afloat. That's where survival skills come in, and trust me, they're just as crucial.

Opening a Business

Survival skills in business is a whole different craft unto itself. It's like switching from playing singles tennis to a triathlon—you need a whole new set of skills. The business world requires you to wear many hats, sometimes all at once. And let's be real, it can be overwhelming.

Owning a business involves more than just being good at your core skill. While there are several hats you'll be wearing, let's break it down into the **major roles**:

- **Sales:** You could be the best at what you do, but if you can't sell it, you're going nowhere fast. Sales skills are about understanding your customer's needs and showing them why your product or service is the best solution.
- **Marketing:** From social media to email campaigns, knowing how to market your business is crucial. It's about getting your name out there and creating a buzz.

- **Accounting:** Tracking expenses and write-offs is a task that should remain under the advisement of an expert. Finding your bookkeeper, accountant, CPA and/or your tax strategist is important to do early on. If you have zero saved for taxes, start setting aside 10% of your income for your annual business taxes. You'll need a better plan than this, but do start from day one saving for your quarterly and year-end expenses.

- **Copywriting:** Words matter. Good copy can make or break your marketing efforts. Learning how to write compelling, persuasive copy can significantly boost your engagement and conversion rates. Understanding how to use artificial intelligence can be a game changer as you create masterful copy.

- **Leadership:** Whether you have a team of one or one hundred, leadership skills are essential. It's about inspiring, guiding, and growing your team to achieve more together. If you're a solopreneur, leadership of yourself is just as important.

- **Humility:** Let's face it, we all make mistakes. Being humble enough to admit when you're wrong and learning from those mistakes is a powerful tool for growth.

- **Growth:** Never stop learning. The business world is constantly evolving, and so should you. Stay curious, stay hungry, and keep pushing your boundaries.

Figuring out how to balance these skills on your own can be time-consuming and costly. Mistakes are part of the learning curve, but some mistakes can set you back financially. Here's a pro-tip: seek help. Invest in training, find a mentor, or join a network of fellow entrepreneurs. The greatest power move is realizing that you need help. Believe me, none of us do it all *on our own*. Some of us try and realize that we are really good at certain areas, and we prioritize our time to focus on those profit-generating activities.

The optimal position is having excellent technical skills combined with the ability to confidently run your business. This blend is your secret sauce. While some people possess the ability to do it all, most of us build teams that compensate for our shortcomings. We surround ourselves with experts in their respective roles to create a well-rounded team.

When you master this balance, you're not just surviving—*you're thriving*. In the beginning, you're likely wearing many hats. As soon as you can, consider which roles would be best to delegate.

For me, I started with a personal concierge service to help manage the household. Then, when my business grew enough to support it, I hired a Virtual Assistant. That was when everything leveled up, including my own capabilities.

Remember, you're building a business that's resilient, adaptable, and ready for anything. Having the right team in place makes it much easier to manage everything that comes your way.

Side note from me to you:

If you're reading this and wondering, "What do I do first?" The answer is different for each person. Something tells me that as you look at the list above—and maybe you've added a few more bullet points—there are two that stick out and give you the rapid heartbeat of excitement. Perhaps start there. If your mind can't wrap itself around those ideas, be bold enough to find someone you can hire to train you, someone you can hire to take that part on. Whatever it is for you, do it! We spend too much time waiting for things to change, when the change that needs to happen is within ourselves.

There's no time like the present. Start big. Start small. The most important thing is that you start.

I believe in you.

SOCIAL CAPITAL HIGHLIGHTS

- Technical skills are the backbone of your work.
- Identify the top two business-related skills that keep your heart racing with excitement.
- Search for an expert in that field.
- Keep the faith and continue growing.

Chapter 9

REINVENTING THE WHEEL

The business environment may look different today than it did fifty or even twenty years ago. However, certain ideas stand the test of time. The human experience, when we consider our core, deep values, never truly changes.

Let me share with you some ways this remains relevant.

Everything that's old is new again.

Trends have a way of circling back through and presenting themselves as new, fresh ideas. Bell bottoms went away, then they made a comeback. Songs that were originally released are rerecorded, and for some, hearing them for the very first time, it's like brand-new music.

My dad worked for Ford Motor Company, and he worked long hours to provide for our family. We always ate dinner together at 6:00 p.m. One night, I had heard this really awesome, new song from Pearl Jam. I wanted my parents to hear it because it was one of those songs that told a story. And the story touched my heartstrings.

Pandora didn't exist then. We didn't even have the Google search engine yet! (I'm that old!!) I started singing it—a few bars from the chorus.

And like a miracle ... My dad sang the last line.

I was shocked to learn my dad was cool. I had only heard this song once by dinnertime and here, he knew it, too!

Turned out, he told me that the song originally came out in 1964, and J. Frank Wilson and the Cavaliers sang it first.

The same is true for business. Systems and ideas often cycle back around, as timeless concepts remain relevant. Take handwritten thank-you cards, for example. It's always the right time to send a personalized card to show your gratitude. A golden idea from fifty years ago can still make a significant impact in today's modern business environment.

One Phone Call Away

One day, as a sophomore at Northwood University, I sat down in Miner Hall working away. A phone call came into the office, and Nancy, who answered, called me over when the call was finished. She told me that a call just came in to see if there were any students who would be an ideal fit for what was needed.

She explained that Sali was calling on behalf of her mother, who was elderly and widowed. She was in the hospital and in need of care. Not so much care that she required assistance to live, but someone to pop in and check in on her. Someone to drive her to the grocery store every Friday. A person to take her to her doctors' appointments and take notes so that information wouldn't be missed.

Nancy said, "I think you'd be the best fit for this family," and gave me Sali's phone number.

That one phone call changed my life. The same afternoon, I walked into the hospital room with one single-stem pink rose and met Sali, her sister, and their mother, Dorotha Mae.

For the next three years, I was the person who came to see Dorotha. We would spend Fridays together. We'd stop out for a chicken sandwich from our favorite local shop. We'd watch game shows on the television together. I'd drive her to all of her doctors' appointments. She particularly hated getting her hearing aids checked. Always mild-mannered, Dorotha would have a thing or two to say about the "hearing aid operator" as we left. She'd tell me stories of when her children were younger. She shared with me her love for her grandchildren and great-grandchildren.

During our time together, we got to celebrate Dorotha's eighty-fifth birthday! We threw a beautiful party and decorated in pink and purple, her favorite colors. My time with Dorotha was a blessing.

When my car broke down, it was Dorotha who allowed me to borrow hers while I got mine fixed. It was Dorotha whose companionship meant that neither of us were alone. We had each other during a time when we both needed *someone*.

It didn't seem like a normal trajectory, but that was my job. A job I enjoyed so much. It allowed me to pursue my triple major in International Business, Business Management, and Advertising and finish within four years. After I graduated, I found my replacement, a wonderful younger student at my same university who took over and made sure Dorotha was cared for.

Making an impact on a coworker and being consistent in character opened the door for this opportunity. With literally thousands of students on campus, why did Nancy come straight to me? I would like to think it was because she knew, and was confident, that I could provide the kind, loving, and attentive care that Dorotha's daughters were looking for.

This taught me that every connection, introduction, and relationship has the ability to impact your future. The same is true for your life.

Dorotha Mae is ever-present in my mind. You see, we named our daughter Ellorie Mae after my very dear and special friend.

Alternatives Exist

Finding myself going through instructor training for the Dale Carnegie Course following my graduation from college was a major thrill. I had worked so hard to earn the right to go through instructor training, I could hardly believe I was actually doing it!

Once certified, I was in my very early twenties. A powerhouse of enthusiasm, I'm sure it was hard for some to take me seriously. I am four feet, eleven inches tall, on a strong day. Being small, yet mighty, always resonated with me.

There was a school opening in Charlotte, Michigan that would open its doors to young people who left the traditional school system. This school gave them a way to earn their GED and complete high school. An interesting component of this school was that students would take the Dale Carnegie Course in Human Relations as part of their core curriculum.

Years earlier, I had done an internship with Phil whose wife was starting this school. When I got a call asking if I'd be interested in teaching the Dale Carnegie Course to high school-aged kids seeking to finish their high school education, I couldn't say *YES* fast enough.

My age, experience, and now being a certified instructor gave me the qualifications I needed to meet this task and take it on with gusto. That opportunity wouldn't have been possible had it not been for my relationship as a college freshman interning for Phil and keeping those relationships open.

Music to My Ears

My mother was a music minister for our church, starting in sixth grade at her Catholic school as one of the few kids who could play the piano. Her love of music significantly influenced my own passion for music and worship.

Following in her footsteps, I became a music minister after getting my driver's license. I was hired at three churches, playing for the 5:00 and 7:00 p.m. masses on Saturdays and 9:00 and 11:00 a.m. masses on Sundays. This continued throughout high school.

Once in college, I became a substitute for other music ministers and jumped back to full time once I landed after college.

Here's the kicker. This really amazing guy I was dating (and ultimately married) bought us our first home in Plymouth, Michigan. This was "the city" compared to where I grew up in rural Michigan. Twenty miles up the street there was St. Damien of Molokai Parish in Pontiac. The head pastor needed a music minister. And wouldn't you know it, we were raised in that same, tiny parish in

Emmett, Michigan. He had called my mom asking if I ever moved somewhere and if I could help out.

I worked happily for his parish for years.

Seven years later, another phone call came from St. Valentine Catholic Parish that was only eight miles from our home. A priest who worked with my mom in the past had been relocated, and they were in need of a music minister to work with their children's choir.

If you believe in matches made in heaven, *this is one of them.*

Just about the time we were getting married and opening Ryan's business, this change of venue came my way.

St. Valentine had a kindergarten-through-eighth grade school, and they needed a music minister to lead that program.

The Lord works in mysterious ways. Having had all this experience with adult choirs and a natural desire to work with younger kids, this brought all of my passions together. For eight years, I led the St. Valentine Children's Choir and grew that program into a vital part of the parish.

Teaching a group of third through eighth graders to sing and lead a congregation in praise and worship was the epitome of *"Best Job Ever!"*

Ryan and I got married at this parish. Our daughter, Ellorie, was baptized there. It was my privilege to serve these communities.

Neither of these roles would have been possible without my being referred to them. I never had to interview. These opportunities were made available to me due to the existing relationships that were formed and maintained throughout the years.

St. Valentine Children's Choir

From a Room I Wasn't In

Who is saying *your name* in rooms that you're not in?

Here is the most important takeaway on how growing your social capital impacts business. Building social capital is like having an army out in the field, spotting opportunities for you and bringing you up in conversation in rooms you're not even in.

The skill of being a top-notch referral partner is one that is a give and take. Both parties have to benefit.

In 2010, I had been busy growing my consultancy business, Dynamisis, LLC. We focused on helping generational family businesses during the time of transitioning from one generation to the next. Our specialty was bridging the gap of communication between the outgoing owner (usually a grandpa or a dad) to their grandson, or son.

I have always been fond of professional development and corporate training. During this season of life, I threw myself into gaining as much experience and expertise as I could. I became a certified BNI Director and Trainer and an instructor for Dale Carnegie Training and earned my DiSC® Trainer Certification.

In the meantime, as I was building my experience and expanding my social capital, I received a phone call from someone I met through BNI. A nearby Christian college had been looking for a professor to teach their freshman level Fundamentals of Speech Communication class.

They said that I could work under the guidance of the department head. This was important because I didn't have a master's degree to teach at the collegiate level. They found a way! For the next two years, I taught college students that public speaking was something they should run toward not away from.

This was a role that I never sought out, but it came looking for me. Somewhere, in a room I wasn't in, someone heard of a need, and they thought *I'd be a perfect fit* to solve it.

Sometimes, we meet someone, and the energy is dynamic and we feel an instant connection.

Other times, it's a slow burn.

Then there are times when we build a relationship over time that is based on mutual respect.

The point is, no matter how your relationships begin, establishing your social capital takes intentional activity and interaction with other people—consistently and genuinely.

As you launch your business, you'll find you're going to be invited to events you've never attended or asked to go to a group you've never heard of before. Instead of playing it safe, I encourage you to say "Yes" to new things!

Every person that played a major role in my life was, at one time, a stranger.

SOCIAL CAPITAL HIGHLIGHTS

- Trends tend to circle back around.
- If you're staying in front of people, you'll remain top of mind when opportunities arise.
- Contacts from your history can make an impact in your present life.
- Every person who plays a major role in your life now was once a stranger.

Chapter 10

IT'S GO TIME!
Target Market and Identifying Your Niche

*I*n today's competitive business landscape, understanding your target market is critical to achieving sustainable growth and success. Identifying your ideal customer demographic allows you to tailor your products or services to meet their specific needs and preferences, increasing the likelihood of attracting and retaining loyal clientele. By focusing on a particular niche within your broader market, you can differentiate yourself from competitors and position your brand as a go-to solution for a distinct audience segment.

When we get specific, we can focus our efforts more directly. This results in spending money more wisely towards marketing, higher conversion rates, and increased customer loyalty.

It may seem counterintuitive, but casting a wider net is way too general. When you help *everyone everywhere* ... you really help no one.

Have you ever asked yourself, "I wonder what I should focus on today for my new post?" When you're talking directly to a specific audience, the narrative continues and grows. It's a beautiful thing to be a part of. The time you spend on creating content for your specific audience allows you to post relevant content to your target market. Your purpose is to create a close connection to them that drives engagement and brand affinity.

When you've done the work to fully identify your true, ideal client, then you're able to talk directly to and attract those specific people.

A client I work with shared her ideal client profile, and it is a perfect example of how specific to get!

Ideal Client: Sara

- Born between 1978 and 1985
- Married with 2 – 4 children
- Loves 80s music
- Knows every *Saved by the Bell* reference possible
- College educated, and hasn't worked for the last five years raising her children
- She desires freedom, being outside, kid-friendly parks, and recreation
- She loves to dance to 80s and 90s music
- Identifies as Carrie not Charlotte, Samantha, or Miranda
- She wishes she could be on vacation all the time but, life

This is all important.

Her ideal client, "Sara," is humanized now. The content and videos that my client makes are now directed to "Sara" every time. There's no confusion over whom she is talking to. She's having a conversation and always keeping "Sara" in the center of her mind. She uses music that Sara would like in her videos, and she uses colors and sounds that are attractive to her and in line with her interests.

How can you take this example and create for yourself what your best, ideal client *really looks like?*

_____

_____

_____

_____

_____

Can you see yourself having a conversation with your best, ideal client, now that you've identified exactly who they are?

Where Are They Online?

Identifying your specific market is important. The next step is to determine *where* they are spending their time and how to engage with them on social media. Each platform is designed differently. How you interact on LinkedIn® is going to be very different than how you engage with your audience on Instagram®.

Using technology to leverage your market research can teach you invaluable insights into the online behavior of your specific target audience. We can't just launch and send out a few posts, like a few stories, and watch our product or idea soar. It takes *strategy*.

Things to consider:

- Which online platforms do they use most?
- What times of day have the highest engagement?
- What length of content is best for this market?
- What is the highest pain point they are trying to overcome?
  - What is your solution?
  - What benefits will they experience using your solution?
  - What stories can you share with others who have had success using your strategy?
  - What did you do BEFORE you knew this strategy?
  - How did you come to realize this strategy works?
  - When they are free from this pain point, how will their life be improved?

These are the types of engagement using your own social media:

- Posting
- Video post
- Advertisements
- Questions with interactive answer feature
- Social media campaigns
- Educational post
- Inspiring post
- Personal insights (from your perspective)

- Reels
- Stories
- Links to articles
- Sharing someone else's post

One additional way to meet your audience where they are is to do a paid advertising campaign that is targeted and directed at a very specific audience. We have so much capability to meet our future clients right where they are ... We just have to understand how to get our message in front of them.

Overcome Negative Impulse

Negative impulse is the feeling that stunts your ability to move forward with your plans and dreams. Positive impulse is the driving force behind what gets you up and out of bed. We thrive when our positive impulse is in motion.

Many people fall victim to acting on their negative impulses which leaves them paralyzed and stalled. When you're building your business, be conscious to move away from these areas that stall your movement:

- Seasonality
- Crazy past clients
- Not knowing how to drive traffic to your social media
- Market saturation
- Lack of training
- Lack of talent
- Self-doubt
- Perfectionism
- Life events

Networking

There is so much information on networking. The best advice is to find your natural cadence and use what works best for you. Then, always improve on it.

Based on building all four of my businesses by word of mouth, I'll share what works for me.

In my course, Bite-Sized Decisions through my company, Social Capital Academy, we go in detail through all of these steps. Engagement in your network at the start of your business feels more like *work* itself. It's something you have to show up for. You have to put the time and energy into it. You have to follow up.

If you're at an event and you're sitting at the table eating by yourself, you're wasting your time. It's not called Netsit. And it's not called Neteat … It's called Network.

Take this quiz on Networking:

                                                                      YES   NO

1. I always have a clear goal of whom I need to meet.

2. I always attend events with a networking partner.

3. I never sell myself or products to people at the event itself.

4. Once I recognize that a person is not a fit for me, I disengage from the conversation respectfully.

YES   NO

5. I understand which professionals are in my power team.

6. I eat before I arrive, so I'm not starving.

7. Once I maximize my time, I leave the event.

8. I always exchange information and "follow" online those I've met and want to reconnect with.

9. In the parking lot, I always send an IM, DM, email, or text to set the follow up with my favorite connections.

10. I prepare an agenda for the follow-up meeting to respect the time and purpose of our meeting.

When I meet with new business owners and discuss these networking ideas, many are surprised. Over time, as you become more efficient with your time, you'll find networking events and gatherings to be valuable opportunities to build your community. While you may have differing opinions on these strategies, the key is to take action.

There have been multiple events where I didn't meet a single person I'd pursue as part of my network, and that's okay!

In my early years of networking, I often attended events with my friend Jenny, who founded A Place for Grace. Jenny's facility is a premier care provider in Saginaw, Michigan, offering fully inclusive educational care for children with special needs.

Isn't it true that we're more likely to believe good things said about someone by others rather than by themselves? Third-party testimonials are far more impactful. Leveraging this truth, attending events with a partner allows you to advocate for each other during introductions and provide additional context. In turn, they introduce you to people and speak on your behalf, creating a powerful and credible impression.

Jenny's work has major impact and the fact it's available in Saginaw means that she can reach families who look for this kind of care for their children. While Jenny has earned every recognition she's received, you can imagine how difficult it would be to sing her own praises. So, I would do that for her. This practice of partnering for events also allows you to have more fun, engage with more people, and successfully turn a night of introductions into a night of new beginnings.

While these ideas may be new to you, I can confirm with confidence that every single idea I list will make you a far more effective networker.

Use this time to practice speaking about yourself and your business. If you have nothing to lose, why not give it all you've got?

Keep in mind these categories of people:

> **Referral Partner:** There's a mutually beneficial relationship and referrals flow from you and to you.
>
> **Power Team:** These are professionals who work with the same clientele but are not your direct competitor. These are the best relationships to build.
>
> **Champions:** Those who promote you because they believe in you and do so willingly.

The people you bring in as part of your networking community are like incredible salespeople. They are in rooms you aren't in and can recognize a good opportunity for you and will bring you up. In much the same way, you must be willing to bring that level of commitment to your relationship, too. This is never a one-way street.

Every time you meet with someone in your network, you're working on strengthening your relationship with each other. Use skill-building exercises and fun stories to help highlight and teach your referral partners what to look for and what to say in those times when opportunities present themselves.

I have a referral partner who specializes in helping women going through divorce make sense out of their financial health and give them confidence to make decisions for their future. This topic can be very sensitive and is an important time for her clients. As a partner to her, I really wanted to know what to say to bring her up in conversation and make it easy.

By asking for that help, she filled me with knowledge and words to use. This made it so much easier for me to speak confidently in those times. When I found opportunities to bring her up in conversation, it resulted in a higher degree of referral.

Building a strong network takes time. I've always aimed to cultivate deep, meaningful relationships rather than shallow, linear connections. I'd rather have six solid bonds with people who share a commitment to mutual goals, introductions, support, and showing up for one another than thirty contacts who won't take my call.

Online relationships require just as much intention and effort. When building online connections, consider how your interactions impact those you're connecting with. Instead of merely "liking" or "loving" a post, send a direct message with a heart and a short note about what you liked. This ensures they read and engage with your words. A simple thumbs-up doesn't carry the same weight.

For example, there's a realtor in Raleigh whose energy radiates through her social media posts. Knowing her now, I see she's the same online as in person. Leonna creates amazing TikTok-style videos, nailing the timing and exuding fierce energy. I learned that sending her direct messages with positive feedback opened the door to us getting to know each other.

As you engage with others, always be mindful of how you're perceived. You may need to adjust your approach until you establish a strong relationship.

SOCIAL CAPITAL HIGHLIGHTS

- **Identify and Focus on Your Niche.** Clearly define your ideal client profile to tailor your products and services to meet their specific needs. Understanding and targeting a specific audience allows you to create more relevant content and marketing strategies, resulting in higher engagement and customer loyalty.

- **Understand Where Your Audience Spends Their Time.** Research and identify the online platforms your target market uses most. Tailor your content and engagement strategies for each platform to maximize reach and interaction. Use analytics and insights to refine your approach continuously.

- **Leverage Social Media Effectively.** Utilize various types of social media engagement such as posts, video content, advertisements, and interactive features. Develop a content calendar and strategy that addresses your audience's pain points and showcases how your solutions can improve their lives.

- **Overcome Negative Impulse.** Recognize and address common obstacles such as self-doubt, perfectionism, and market saturation. Develop a positive mindset and focus on the driving forces that motivate you to move forward with your plans and dreams.

- **Master Networking.** Attend networking events with a clear goal, follow up with contacts, and build mutually beneficial relationships. Focus on creating a network of referral partners, power teams, and champions who can advocate for your business and help you grow. Use each networking opportunity to practice speaking about your business confidently.

Chapter 11

MITIGATE RISK AND FINANCIAL WORRY

*B*uilding a business means pouring your heart, time, and resources into something you believe in, but are you fully protecting what you're working so hard to create? Understanding the ins and outs of insurance might not seem glamorous, but it's a crucial aspect of safeguarding your efforts. As a business owner, staying unaware of the different types of insurance coverage could leave you exposed to significant risks—and potential losses that could have been avoided.

Take it from me: I've seen how quickly things can shift when you're not covered the way you thought you were. Imagine driving to a networking event with a referral partner in your car. If you get into an accident while driving for business purposes, will your personal auto insurance protect you and your passenger? Or would you need a commercial auto policy to be fully covered? And what if a client sues you because they took your business advice, and it resulted in a $35,000 loss on their end? Is your personal liability umbrella policy enough, or do you need a specific General Liability policy for this scenario?

If you can't answer these questions with confidence, this chapter is for you. Understanding the different types of insurance—both personal lines and commercial lines, and the need for specialized policies—can mean the difference between a minor setback and a devastating blow to your personal life and to your business. Let us dig into the details so you can move forward with peace of mind, knowing you're prepared for whatever comes your way.

As a past Insurance Agent, I know firsthand how fast the need for insurance happens because it happened to me. As a freshly-licensed sixteen-year-old, I was the part of the population that makes the statistic true: *brand new drivers have a higher propensity for risk than seasoned drivers.*

It was "Snowcoming" and where I grew up in rural Michigan, it was as big as homecoming. It was just in the winter. The week was full of spirit days, and this particular day was *pajama day!*

There was a four-way stop sign that was the final turn before heading into campus. It was at this intersection, at approximately 7:45 a.m., when my life intersected with more than the road.

While completing my left turn, I felt my car get pushed and rammed from the passenger side rear tire area. It moved my car to a place I was not planning on going. Air bags deployed for the other driver and her front end was wrecked.

Car phones came in bags at that time. I pulled out the bag and turned on this (now ancient) telephonic device and called my mom at home. As it turned out, the other driver was going to call an attorney and what happened next surprised us all.

I learned in this situation that anyone can sue anyone, at any time, for any reason.

For a year and a half, we went through the legal system, as the other driver sued me.

And by suing me (I was 16!) they were really suing my mom and dad.

You see, I was driving *their car*. I was a listed driver on *their auto insurance*. The car was registered *in their name*.

Being sued is energy-draining. It elevates stress in your life and pops in and out of life as your case is processed.

I remember being deposed by opposing council, and they railed me on the fact I used words like "presume" as I spoke about the facts of the four-way intersection where the accident occurred. We went in depth through the intersection "rules of the road."

You see, in a flash, all the details that go by you and are seemingly irrelevant become absolutely relevant. Details like the exact time of the accident. The weather. What was my visibility like? Was I in a hurry?

There are plenty of assumptions that can be made. Remember that I mentioned it was *pajama day* at school? One of the assumptions the police made at the scene—*and put in the report*—was that I must have been in a hurry because I was still wearing pajamas.

Friends, I share this story with you because I learned a lot of lessons during this time. In the end, we were both found 50 percent at fault, and so no payout occurred.

Risk has a way of creeping up on you and making your life very uncomfortable. Had you asked me if I would one day marry a man who was a third-generation insurance agent or become an insurance agent myself, I think we all would have bet against it! Life has a great sense of humor if you allow yourself to see it.

As a professional in this field, those who know me well won't be surprised to see that we will cover how to mitigate risk.

Staying in the dark about your personal insurance needs leaves you exposed to risks that could derail everything you've worked so hard to build. It's easy to assume that your existing coverage will handle whatever comes your way, but when you're operating a business, the stakes are higher, and the needs are different. Without understanding the specific insurance requirements for your business—like whether your personal auto policy covers you when driving to a meeting with a client or if you need a separate General Liability policy for business-related claims—you're leaving yourself vulnerable to potential financial losses.

Taking the time to get informed puts you in the proverbial driver's seat, giving you control over how well-protected your business truly is. By being proactive about your insurance needs, you're not just avoiding unnecessary risks—you're ensuring that you have the right safety nets in place so that you can focus on growth and building something lasting.

In business and life, you have the ability to understand what options you have so that you can decide what you need.

Key Terms to Help Mitigate Risk

Homeowners Insurance is designed to rebuild and/or replace your home if there were a total loss. This policy comes with coverage for:

Structure of your home: walls, floors, roof (also called Coverage A)

Other Structures: fence, deck, patio, firepit, barns, etc.

Personal Property: every article of clothing, furniture, décor, etc.

Personal Liability: if someone is injured while on your property (guest, vendor, trespasser)

Deductible is the amount you pay yourself and, if the claim is covered, your insurance policy would cover the balance.

- **Specific Amount Deductible**   **$2,500**

- **Percentage Deductible**   1% refers to 1% of the Coverage A amount on your policy.

Automobile Insurance covers you and those listed on your policy with the following types of coverage. *This can change state by state, so always confirm with your personal agent as to how your policy is specifically designed for your family.*

Bodily Injury Liability   **250 / 500 / 100**

This is protection available to cover the injuries, loss of income, loss of use or dismemberment of another driver or other passengers in a vehicle.

The numbers mean:

250   Your policy covers you for $250,000 maximum per one person, individually.

500   Your policy covers you for $500,000 maximum per accident, regardless of how many people may be injured or are suing you.

100   Your policy has $100,000 to cover property damage.

Underinsured / Uninsured Motorist Coverage covers *you* if the person on the other side of the accident may be <u>under</u>insured or is <u>un</u>insured.

Personal Liability Umbrella Policy is how you increase your amount of liability insurance that will cover you personally and all who are in your household. This comes in $1,000,000 increments. This is the best and most reasonably priced option for businesspeople. This is a recommended option because liability insurance acts like a cushion between you, an accident, and the need to liquidate your own personal assets.

*The size of your cushion is up to you.

Life Insurance is protection for your family or anyone who relies on you for care and financial support. This can be purchased in a variety of ways. The two most popular are:

> **Term Life Insurance**: It provides coverage for a specific amount of time (ten years, twenty years, or thirty years, for example). The price stays the same and does not increase over time. You can normally acquire more life insurance at a lower cost using term insurance.

Pro Tip: If you are considering that you'll need coverage for twenty years or more, it is better to get the longer term at the start of your policy period. When it comes time to buy a new term policy, your rate will change based on several factors, *plus*, if anything in your health has changed, you may no longer be eligible for coverage. Always seek the advice from your personal insurance agent to ensure your family is properly protected.

Whole Life Insurance: This is life insurance that will never expire or end, so long as the premiums are paid. This is usually a bit more expensive, and therefore, it's difficult to get higher amounts of insurance.

Life insurance has several elements to consider. Cash Value is a big topic people like to investigate. Ultimately, life insurance is not an investment. It's a tool to protect your family against the unexpected loss of life of a providing family member.

General Liability Insurance is what businesses need to protect against being sued for their professional activities or advice. This type of insurance is commonly referred to as **Business Owner's Policy/ Commercial Insurance Policy.**

Every business from manufacturing, restaurateurs, consultants, tree trimmers, landscaping companies, and real estate agents to heating and cooling companies need to have a general liability insurance policy. This is the policy that will protect you, as a business owner, from risk associated to your professional activities.

The Difference Between Knowing and Hoping

Mitigating risk and establishing proper insurance is a part of life many are willing to take a backseat on.

We entrust others to make choices for us while we cling to the phrase "I didn't know!" to get us out of guilt for not taking a leadership role in our own life.

There's a vast difference between having certainty and merely wishing for it.

It's time to bid farewell to our old companion, apathy. Think of her as a former friend we've outgrown and now realize isn't beneficial for us anymore. We let her go so we can grow. No one ever grows while being complacent.

Budgeting for Rainy Days

If you're at the stage where you still have a full-time role and are starting your business on the side, this is for you!

If you're ready to jump into your passion project with both feet, this is for you!

Be mindful and strategic about how you manage your business income.

1. Put profits first
2. Invest now in your future
3. Prepare for unforeseen expense
4. Mitigate risk through insurance choices

Put Profits First

In his book, *Profit First: How to Transform Your Business from a Cash-Eating Monster to a Money-Making Machine*, Mike Michalowicz flips the traditional accounting equation of "Sales - Expenses = Profit" to "Sales - Profit = Expenses."[1] This simple change in mindset encourages businesses to allocate profit first, ensuring profitability from the outset. By setting aside a predetermined percentage of income as profit, businesses force themselves to operate within their means.

Profit First provides a practical, actionable system that helps business owners prioritize profitability and gain control over their finances. By reallocating funds and changing financial habits, businesses can achieve long-term success and stability.

Invest Now in Your Future

Your business will have different needs in its second year, third year, and beyond. Set aside resources now to prepare for those future demands. If hiring a virtual assistant could positively impact your life, schedule, and outcomes, don't delay. Failing to expand quickly enough to support your growth could result in a significant loss, potentially costing you $100,000.

---

[1] Michalowicz, Mike. *Profit First: Transform Your Business from a Cash-Eating Monster to a Money-Making Machine.* Penguin, 2017.

Prepare for Unforeseen Expenses

If your business is the sole provider for your family, consider starting a separate account designed for times you need it. An air conditioning unit, furnace, medical bills, and new set of tires can all add up. It's easier to set a little aside than it is to find a large chunk. Your growth stage in business will have months of amazing growth and some months making you ask, *"What just happened?"*

You've Got this

People don't struggle with thinking too big. They struggle with thinking too small. There are resources available to help you think bigger, dream bigger, and act with more confidence. Google it, YouTube it—whatever you do, equip yourself with the tools needed to act. How would you behave if you knew you couldn't fail? Timidity isn't a friend to business owners.

As you build your social capital, I challenge you to have conversations about ideas, overcoming challenges, and training your mind to see situations with a mindset of "How can I handle this?" instead of "There's no way I can get through this." The key difference lies in putting this mindset into practice.

SOCIAL CAPITAL HIGHLIGHTS

- **Anyone can sue you at any time for any reason.** Surround yourself with experts in the field of insurance who will advise you and assist you in leveraging your best approach to protecting yourself and safeguarding your future.

- **Understand and Mitigate Risk.** Gain a thorough understanding of various types of insurance such as homeowners, automobile, life, and general liability insurance. Protect yourself and your business by ensuring you have the appropriate coverage to mitigate potential risks and financial liabilities.

- **Embrace Financial Responsibility.** Prioritize financial planning by setting aside profits first, as suggested by the *Profit First* methodology. This ensures that your business remains profitable and financially stable from the outset. Allocate a percentage of income as profit before covering expenses.

- **Prepare for Unforeseen Expenses.** Establish a separate savings account for unexpected expenses. Regularly contribute to this fund to cover potential emergencies like medical bills or essential repairs, ensuring that your business can weather financial challenges without significant disruption.

- **Invest in Your Future.** Consistently invest in your future by contributing to retirement funds or other long-term investment accounts. Strategic planning and regular contributions will ensure financial security and comfort in the years to come.

- **Replace Doubt with Certainty.** Take an active leadership role in understanding and managing your risks and finances. Move away from relying on others to make decisions for you, and gain confidence in your choices by being well-informed and proactive about your financial and risk management strategies.

Chapter 12

YOUR SOCIAL CAPITAL BEGINS WITH YOU

As we round out our time together, let's focus on the type of person you are.

Your behaviors, attitude, and personality will be what draws people your way.

Both online and in person, we have to share the vibe that will attract our tribe.

If you're online looking for ways to go viral and duplicate what you see someone else doing but yours falls flat, it's probably because it wasn't true to you. Don't chase virality! The best thing about you is your own special and unique energy. How you do things is different. That's what makes you interesting. Remember to be you as you show people who you are, both online and in person.

Here are the behaviors and attributes that help magnetize people towards you. Your ability to build social capital begins with you.

There are two types of skills: *interpersonal* skills and *intra-personal* skills. These two skill sets are fundamental for building successful relationships—both with others and within yourself.

Interpersonal Skills

Interpersonal skills refer to your ability to interact and communicate effectively with others, both verbally and non-verbally.

These habits are important to have:

- Showing respect for, understanding, and empathizing with other people's emotions and perspectives.
- Effective listening, clear communication, and conflict resolution are central to interpersonal skills.
- Building rapport, networking, and collaboration skills are essential in business settings.

Strong interpersonal skills foster positive relationships with customers, clients, team members, and your overall network around you. They contribute to a supportive and harmonious work environment, enhancing teamwork and productivity.

Intrapersonal Skills

Intrapersonal skills pertain to your understanding and management of your own emotions, motivations, and behaviors.

These habits are important to have:

- Self-awareness, self-regulation, and resilience in the face of challenges.

- Goal setting, positive self-talk, managing your time wisely, and decision-making, all aspects of intrapersonal skills crucial for personal and professional growth.

- Emotional intelligence (EI) and keeping your emotions moderate so you can enjoy the high points and learn to navigate through the low points.

As a solopreneur, it has always been my experience that whatever the outcome of the day or event, it's been a direct correlation to the amount of dedicated energy and positive effort I put into it. Surely, when you're approaching an appointment and you're filling your mind with the type of negative talk that would make a sailor blush, you can't be surprised when you didn't show up as your best self during the appointment.

Developing relationships with others is best when the relationship we have with ourselves is one of respect and appreciation, sprinkled with just enough risk to keep us on our toes.

The benefit of working to develop your intrapersonal skills is managing stress in a way that it doesn't overtake your mind and crush your spirit. It also allows you to stay motivated and maintain a positive mindset as you build off your new ideas. The confidence you get as a result of truly liking yourself is something people can recognize when they meet you.

Just as you can pick up when someone is arrogant, or feels entitled, smug or rude—they don't have to wear a name badge declaring it. It comes across very prominently upon meeting them. So, too, does confidence in yourself. It empowers you to make informed decisions and take ownership of your actions.

The freedom that comes from personal responsibility is powerful. Self-reliance is a huge motivator. When all of the outcomes are reliant on your own personal actions, you become interested in seeing things through and are open to trying things a different way if they could improve the outcome. The openness your mind experiences allows for breakthroughs that span your marriage, friendships, parenting, and how you show up in the world outside of your business.

As you build and grow your business, honing both interpersonal and intrapersonal skills will be key to fostering meaningful connections with others and cultivating a resilient and adaptive entrepreneurial mindset. Remember, investing in these skills not only enhances your professional capabilities, but also contributes to a fulfilling and rewarding journey as a business owner.

The Tenets of Being Your Own Boss

Protect yourself from burnout by focusing your attention on these areas first:

Learn How to Say No. Empower yourself by setting expectations on what you will and will not do. Being a *"yes person"* doesn't leave you with much energy left in your own bucket. Be intentional about how you invest your time and skills and with whom you invest them. Early in the years of your business, you'll need to carve out time to meet people and establish relationships. All of this is good.

Be mindful of your generosity, and don't give too much of yourself until you know if it's going to be time (or money) well spent. In my line of work, I received calls all the time looking for money towards sponsoring things that I was not connected to. If you need a way to respond, here's an option that doesn't allow for a follow-up: *Thank you for calling. This year's sponsorship budget has already been allocated. Best wishes in finding your sponsors.*

You Do Not Exist Just to Look Pretty. Your value goes beyond appearances, let your impact shine. Showing up for people and sharing yourself and your world is a big step in sharing your message with your ideal clients. Sometimes people think they have to be perfect and do everything with the absolute best lighting to begin. That's simply untrue. To start, you simply have to show up. Show up as you are.

Trust me, who you are comes across clearly when it's just you talking to the person you've identified as your ideal client. They need you. They are experiencing a hardship or are struggling in a certain area of their life. Because of the business you've created and are building, they are going to find a way out.

While branding is important, don't focus on it so much that all you become is a "pretty face." Ground yourself in value. That is always best.

Practice Being Unoffendable. Build resilience by not taking things personally. When I launched my first business back in 2006, I thought I had identified the missing piece to what kept family-run businesses from transitioning between generational family members with ease. What I found out is that while my hunch was correct, I needed to take in more practical information and pivot my approach. Had I been offended by how my offer wasn't accepted upon being presented, I would have missed out on improving the process.

We all have to deal with keyboard warriors. That will be a part of your future if you decide to promote and market yourself online.

Someone once told this to me, and it helps create space for messages and comments that seemed way off base:

> *"Online is a place where people gather and leave*
> *their passing thoughts then they move on. Their comments*
> *are not rooted in truth. Their comments don't need*
> *a permanent place in your mind."*

Give Yourself and Everyone Around You Grace. Practice patience and kindness. You've probably heard the phrase, "Everyone is fighting battles you can't see. Be kind." As I get older, I realize more and more how knowing so much of what is happening in people's lives has torn down our ability to really relate and talk to others when we see them in person. Have you noticed that?

Instead of eagerly asking what has been happening in their life, when we see someone, we try to recall what we've seen them post recently. Most of real life doesn't get shown on *Reel Life*. The antidote, I've found, is to stay curious. Ask people to share their life and adventures with you. You'll find the sincerest part of who they are shines when they speak about the people and times that are most important to them.

If you have an event and someone cancels on you, choose grace. If you have a lunch date and they are late or a no-show, choose grace. You'll never regret it when you give it. It is the times when we don't give it and use harsh judgment that we often regret our actions.

Leave regret out of your life. Practice grace, and give it to others freely.

Someone Else's Green Grass is Probably Astroturf. Focus on your unique path instead of envying others. Once you find your lane in business, push forward with your own unique approach. While it's always good to get anecdotal evidence and do industry research, never make yourself a copy of someone else's strength. You have your own!

You Don't Have to Wait for an Apology to Forgive. Free yourself from grudges and move forward. There will be people you bring into your life who may let you down. There will be people who promise they have your back, but you find they are unable to live up to their promises.

I hired a videographer back in my early years of business. (Back then, cell phones didn't have cameras and weren't a part of capturing our everyday life.) There was a major training I had to conduct, and it was a big account. I got permission from the client to record the session and use it in the future for my own marketing. The training day came, and all the footage was collected.

When two weeks went by and I didn't hear back from the videographer, I called. Left messages. Sent text messages. Nothing! He was either dodging me or in the hospital. The social network known as Facebook was very young at this time. Fortunately, I had it because I had been in college a few years earlier *and so had this guy.*

I learned a valuable lesson. If you want people to contact you, make it to their benefit to do so.

I posted to his page a message something like this:

> *Has anyone heard from Larry? I've been calling and trying to connect, and I am very worried about him. Is he okay?*

Guess how quickly Larry called me.

He said he had gotten overwhelmed by the amount of work he had and would call me back in a week to give a timeline of when I would get the tape back.

Well, it's seventeen years later, and I still haven't heard back.

While I will never get an apology or my money back (or my tape, for that matter), I didn't have time to harbor ill will. Being slighted and treated poorly isn't a ticket to a winning game. Let go of letdowns. Don't pack them up and bring them with you. They weigh too much to carry.

You Will Never Make Yourself Look Good by Making Someone Else Look Bad. Lift others up instead of tearing them down. Now that you're a protector of your own business and personal brand, decide how you'd like to be remembered by people who just met you. You have two major options. Are you a person who lifts people up and talks them up in a room they may not be in? Or are you a person who tears people down in the hope that it will make you look good?

If your life were a test on how many lives you can impact, which category would you have the most names in? The good impact or the bad impact?

You have the ability to do so much good with your business. You can help people solve their issue. You can give them ideas that will elevate their thought process. Pouring into people is a way to make a good name for yourself.

It's Never Too Late to Be Exactly Who You Want to Be.
Embrace your potential and pursue your dreams relentlessly.
When I turned forty, it was like my life shifted. I almost immediately started seeing things through a difference lens. All of a sudden, I started realizing that forty years had passed and I wasn't promised forty more.

At the time, I owned my insurance agency. As a franchise, I didn't "work" for anyone, but my office was in Raleigh which was a part of the larger regional territory. We had a new territory manager whom I had never spoken with in the several months since his position change.

I remember it clearly ...

Like any sales organization, the managers are always focused on numbers. Outcomes and results are tracked, and there are spreadsheets and ideas on how to do more and reach higher. All of that never impacted me. I have never been motivated by sales numbers. I'm also not super impressed by it either. I've met many successful people whose company I couldn't keep after three minutes of talking to them.

One email changed everything.

This email, while not remarkable, hit me hard. It had the normal *Rah-rah, let's beat the Southeast Territory this week. Push hard. Sell hard. Get up at 5:00 a.m., work out, start calling by 7:00 a.m., don't stop calling until after 7:00 p.m. ...* You know the drill.

Then he signed off with this phrase:

LFGI

The first letter meant "Let's."

The last two letters meant "Get It."

You can fill in the blank.

I read that a few times and **knew**. This was not a place for me. This no longer served me, and I could no longer be a part of this environment. The good I was aiming to do by helping new home-buyers to find insurance for their new home prior to closing was being tarnished by the part of the business that was all numbers and results ... and no personality.

Within sixty days, I sold my business.

I was retired for thirty-two minutes.

Then it hit me. I have so much passion inside my bones. When I sought out what lights me up and what I can talk about for hours on end, it became clear to me that I still had more in me to give.

In June 2024, I launched a new version of myself and applied the same concepts in this book that allowed me to successfully launch my three other businesses. This time, the difference is the medium by which my products and services can be experienced. The shift in approach required new learning. I've never used email funnels, never done evergreen content, didn't have to rely solely on social media for wide-expansion efforts.

Business, at its core, is based on the same principles across indus-tries. The part that makes it stand out is *you!* Your contribution to your brand is what makes *what* you do and *how* you do it so special.

Learn How to Truly Serve Others. Success comes from helping others succeed. If you were to offer to help your neighbor pick up grass clippings and sweep up their sidewalk, how would they feel about you? Doing something nice for someone else helps that person, and it also helps you. The goodness you feel by helping boosts your oxytocin levels and makes you feel emotionally connected and bonded.

Acts of kindness stick with people. They never forget when you showed up for them.

Apply this to building your brand.

As you meet people, look for opportunities to support them. Show that their priorities matter to you by taking actions that make them feel valued and cared for. Demonstrate through your actions that their wellbeing is important to you and that they are a priority in your life.

Whenever possible, give more than you're asked.

People won't ever forget it.

Control Your Emotions or They Will Control You. Mastering your emotions is crucial for making sound decisions. You know that familiar sensation when anger, frustration, or anxiety begins to rise. For me, it feels like my skin is tingling, almost as if it's on fire. Then, my narrow focus takes over, and my quick tongue can cause more trouble than a match in a fireworks factory. If I don't recognize the surge of my emotions, I can easily explode, hurting those around me. It's my obligation to respond with sensitivity, so when I realize I can't offer my best, I remove myself from the situation.

During times of high emotion, I've found it best to remove myself from the environment. If I'm at home, I go for a walk with my dogs. If I'm in the car, I'll stop by a grocery store and pick up a few regular items to distract myself.

Music has always been a source of emotional breakthrough for me. As a theater kid who loves musicals, my deep love of music started in childhood—I could sing the entire CATS soundtrack with all the emotion it demands! When my nerves are frayed or my emotions are about to burst, I turn on my music. I have a playlist for every situation.

In my experience, while it's rare, if I reach a high level of anger and heightened emotions, the most powerful antidote is immense gratitude.

To push beyond the feeling of powerlessness and rage, I reflect on the moments in my life that fill me with deep and profound gratitude. Then, I play the sixteenth song on the *Mamma Mia! Here We Go Again* soundtrack, allowing myself to truly feel and experience that gratitude. (If you haven't seen the movie to understand the context of this song, I highly recommend it.) The love and emotion that this song evokes in me are indescribable, touching me at the very core of my being.

As I hear the words sung, they make me reflect on my deep and unending love for my daughter. The song is so beautifully written and performed that it evokes the truest feelings of love within me. When I listen to it, any frustration or anger I may have been feeling disappears, leaving me with a significantly improved mood and renewed mental strength.

Gratitude and love always drive out anger and frustration.

If You Can't See the Positive, Be the Positive. Create positivity and inspire others through your actions. Some days positive mindsets come easy. If you had a new client come on board and if it's a Friday, you have a double-winning day!

The true test of building the character trait of being a positive-minded person comes from being able to see the good throughout the storm.

It was almost impossible to see the good when I was three months into my new insurance agency. We had just moved to Raleigh and the pandemic was in full force. Everything was shut down. No one could meet in person. There were no events. I had a sizeable franchise fee that needed to be paid, whether I wrote new business or not.

There were months when I didn't write enough new business to pay all the expenses. Those months when we paid that franchise fee out of our own pockets felt horrible. Those initial months I didn't even want to look at the compensation statement because I knew as soon as I did that my day would turn sour, and that it would take a lot to turn my mind around.

I gave myself a certain time frame to feel crappy. That time frame was that I had to be over my pity party by 5:30 p.m. so my night with my family wasn't ruined by my attitude.

Protect and prioritize the people in your life over the fleeting emotions you may experience as you embark on the journey of owning your own business. Always let your love for those around you overshadow any momentary negative feelings you might have.

Fear Does Not Stop Death, It Stops Life. Overcome fear to truly live and achieve. The irony is that fear never stops the thing you're fearful of from happening. However, in the meantime, it sure ruins your chance at building a life you love. Fear and doubt kill more dreams than failure ever will.

Fear has a new meaning for me. After my daughter was born, something inside of me completely shifted. I had a very difficult pregnancy, and afterwards, my body was rebelling. Part of the revolt included a new fear: the fear of heights and a fear of flying.

I love to travel. I've flown to Japan and Europe. I've traveled more extensively than most people do in a lifetime. But all of a sudden, fear—the type that makes you do things you otherwise wouldn't—was in full control.

In flight, I would have major panic attacks if there was even the slightest bit of turbulence. I would scream out terrible words and lose my ability to control my breathing. This was embarrassing to anyone flying with me. And it was a terrible way to live. As soon as we touched down, I went back to being myself, and the heightened anxiety left.

Recently, my husband and I took our daughter, Ellorie, to the "*Wizard of Oz* Experience" in the mountains of North Carolina. I bought the tickets and knew we would have to ride a ski lift up the mountain. Sometimes, fear has a way of sneaking up on us.

As soon as we sat down on the ski lift, my fear kicked in strongly, making for a very uncomfortable and unpleasant ride. In the midst of it, my husband and daughter reassured and comforted me. My daughter even sang to me, which never happens! Despite fear controlling my mind, I'm so glad I was able to look beyond it and embrace the good around me. I could have missed all the sweetness had I only focused on the fear.

In business, we face many fears. Fear and anxiety can keep us sharp but only if they aren't the primary drivers of our emotions.

Don't Take Social Media Too Seriously. Use it wisely, but don't let it define you. Living your life and sharing what you're comfortable sharing is a good place to start. If you're a naturally funny person, don't keep your sense of humor a secret! If you're naturally shy, don't try to be super outgoing. Everyone has a cadence to speaking. Find yours.

When I taught the fundamentals of speech communication at a local college, I set out to teach my students to find their voice as they began practicing the art of public speaking.

Did you ever think of the fact that your voice is an instrument? Anyone who plays a musical instrument will tell you that it takes constant practice to get to a level where you can play comfortably. It's a whole different level to play without music and improvise.

I know this to be true. As a pianist and organist, I can assure you that most people don't have the ability to sit down on the first day and play anything coherently, much less in the same key.

Be wise and realize as you begin to show up on social media talking about yourself, your business, and how you can help, that others have a lot more practice than you do. Resist the temptation to compare yourself to someone else. You can't compare your first attempts to another professional's many years of training and mastery.

Hold Your Shoulders Back When You Walk Into Every Room. Enter every situation with confidence and on purpose. Confidence is a good thing. Confidence can be a result of time-tested results and experience, or a list of highly satisfied clients. It can also come from a place that's based on passion, determination, grit, and a never-ending spirit.

A friend of mine always said the fact that she never went to college was a reason people wouldn't do business with her. She thought not having a degree was more important than her desire to provide a much-needed service.

The school of real life is a great teacher. Someone who has the tenacity to figure it out and learn will outwork anyone who relies solely on a degree as a testament to their abilities.

Walk into every function you attend like you are meant to be there.

Greet people with eye contact. That act pulls them in. Offer the best warm smile you have. The cool thing about offering a smile first is that most of the time, the person will give one back to you.

If You Think You Can't, You Won't. But If You Think You Can, You Will. Believe in your abilities, and act with conviction. Being willing to figure things out is a core tenet to owning your own business. You wear so many hats as a self-employed business owner. Remember to put on your hat of tenacity daily.

Your mindset shapes your reality. If you think you won't succeed, you'll find a way to prove yourself right. So, for the fun of it, believe that you can succeed—and prove yourself right.

The Loudest People in the Room Are Never the Smartest. Value wisdom and thoughtfulness over noise. Remember to trust your own instincts. Your vision for your business isn't the same as everyone else's. How one person grows their business may not be a good match for the people you are targeting. Stay focused on your ideal client. If you know them, what they need, and what struggles they're experiencing, and you can help them solve it, *don't hesitate.* Move toward them with every single step you take!

SOCIAL CAPITAL HIGHLIGHTS

- **Build Strong Interpersonal Skills.** Develop habits such as showing respect, empathy, effective listening, clear communication, and conflict resolution. Focus on building rapport, networking, and collaboration skills to foster positive relationships and create a supportive work environment.

- **Cultivate Intrapersonal Skills.** Enhance your self-awareness, self-regulation, and resilience. Practice goal setting, positive self-talk, time management, and decision-making. Develop emotional intelligence to manage stress, stay motivated, and maintain a positive mindset.

- **Set Clear Boundaries and Learn to Say No.** Empower yourself by setting boundaries to protect your energy and time. Be intentional with your commitments and prioritize tasks and relationships that align with your goals. Avoid overcommitting to prevent burnout.

- **Show Up Authentically.** Focus on adding value beyond appearances. Be present and genuine in your interactions with clients. Don't strive for perfection; instead, show up as your true self and connect with your audience on a deeper level.

- **Build Resilience and Embrace Challenges.** Practice being unoffendable and learn from setbacks. Approach challenges with a growth mindset and see them as opportunities to improve. Develop strategies to handle criticism and stay focused on your long-term goals.

- **Practice Grace and Patience.** Show kindness and patience to yourself and others. Give grace when others make mistakes or face difficulties. Cultivate a forgiving attitude to free yourself from grudges and move forward positively.

- **Focus on Your Unique Path.** Avoid comparing yourself to others. Embrace your unique strengths and approach to business. Stay true to your vision and concentrate on serving your ideal clients with authenticity and dedication.

Chapter 13

METRICS AND MASTERY

*U*nlocking the keys to building your business in a technical age starts with understanding how you can scale your business using new applications and online platforms. I certainly remember the days of the rotary card files and dialing for appointments. The good news is those techniques are still used by many businesses. If that's your preferred approach, this chapter won't help you.

If you're looking for insights on what resources are available to you now to grow and scale your business, read on, my friend.

Build an Email Distribution List

Think about this. If your online social profiles have a million friends or followers and that platform locks you out of your profile or your profile gets hacked and you cannot retrieve it, is having that many followers really something you can rely on?

When my husband's profile was hacked, we tried every possible way to get it back. We landed on a site on the dark web that said that if we paid them, they guarantee they'll get it back. We didn't believe them and didn't fall for it. He had to start over. Many people find themselves in that situation with their professional profiles, and there is nothing that can be done other than to start over.

Do you realize when you visit an online store for the first time, a pop-up ad shows up on your screen, offering you ten to fifteen percent off of your first order after you provide them with your email address? That's because they understand email distribution lists are an asset they own.

Email distribution lists are lists you actively build and retain.

The ways you use your lists include, but are not limited to:

- Use promotions to your direct target audience
- Engage and add value to nurture your relationships
- Highlight your business demographic analytics
- Launch new products/services to your target niche
- Increase your return business
- Build your visibility and credibility with your closest client base
- Understand where in the market you have become dominant

How Do You Build an Email List?

Lead Magnet Giveaway

How you do it can reflect your style and business. If you're online and using social media, the easiest and most effective approach is to create valuable content and give it away as a lead magnet. If you are seeing the caption: "Comment GUIDE below to get my free guide on how to make the best summer smoothies," then you've already witnessed how successful this approach is.

Some examples of what valuable content could be:

- *Free Guidebook*
- *Top Ten Favorite Tools to Accomplish {the goal}*
- *E-book*
- *E-course*
- *Excel spreadsheet*
- *Digital formatted resources*
- *30-day challenges*
- *Top Hooks to Go Viral Online*

The best application to use to create these would be Canva. The free version is a good place to start. The professional dashboard that you pay for offers a lot more than their free version. If you need a place to start, free is always the right price.

Landing Page

The landing page has essentially replaced a website. It's a stand-alone page designed to specifically market your offers (products, promotions, services). Your prospects arrive on your landing page after following a link—whether provided on social media, an email, post, or online advertisement. Unlike a website's homepage which leads you to multiple locations and purposes, the sole purpose of a landing page is to convert visitors into leads and customers.

Components of a Landing Page:

- **Clear and Compelling Headline.** The headline should immediately grab the attention of the reader and clearly state the value proposition or the main benefit you provide, teach, or offer.

- **Very Focused Content.** Brevity wins the day here. Be concise and direct as to the offer and what you provide.

- **Highly Visual Design.** High-quality images are a reflection of a well-thought-out landing page. Quality images and videos help to enhance the impact and make the page more engaging.

- **Call to Action (CTA).** This statement is prominently displayed and persuasive. There is usually an "act now" button with a phrase that's engaging and empowering. This is how you guide the visitor to take the desired action.

- **Building Trust.** Testimonials, reviews, or trust badges help build credibility and reassure visitors that your offer is safe and full of value.

Benefits of Landing Pages:

- **Remove Distractions.** Removing the distractions of websites and funneling people into a powerfully worded single-page landing site significantly improves the chances of converting leads into customers.

- **More Cost Effective.** The cost of creating a landing page is far less than building out, designing, and hosting a full website. When landing pages are optimized properly, they have impressive results and make a huge impact on a business's marketing plan.

- **Provide Clarity.** The unnecessary elements that take people away from the primary goal are all removed by using this approach. You provide clarity which streamlines your marketing efforts and allows you to measure success more accurately.

- **Copy Matters.** Keep in mind how you write your copy for the landing page. A well-designed page can boost search engine rankings and improve performance of online ads based on the words used. By ensuring that the landing page content aligns closely with the ad or search query, your business can achieve better ad quality scores and lower cost per click, depending on the type of ads you run.

Utilizing Funnels and Automation

Funnels are the backbone of a successful marketing strategy. They guide prospective customers through a process—from awareness to decision-making and, in the end, conversion.

Main Elements of Funnels:

Awareness	Attract visitors with value-driven content
Interest	Engage them with informative emails and social media posts
Decision	Nurture leads with targeted offers and testimonials to build your brand
Action	Convert leads into customers with a compelling Call to Action (CTA)

Applications to Consider:

ChatGPT is an advanced language model developed by OpenAI. It leverages deep learning to understand and generate human-like text, making it useful for a wide range of applications, from customer support to creative writing. It provides users with an interactive and intelligent assistant capable of understanding context and generating relevant responses.

Google Analytics tracks and analyzes the performance of your landing pages and funnels. It provides in-depth insights into user behavior, helping you identify areas for improvement.

FloDesk is an excellent tool for building and managing your email list. Its user-friendly interface and beautiful email templates make it easy to create and send professional-looking emails. Use FloDesk's analytics to track open rates, click-through rates, and overall engagement to provide valuable insights into your audience's preferences.

FloDesk Analytics are FloDesk's built-in analytics that offer valuable data on email performance, allowing you to optimize your email campaigns for better engagement and conversions.

ClickFunnels is an all-in-one tool for building and managing marketing funnels. It simplifies the process of creating sales pages, webinars, and automated email sequences. Use ClickFunnels to design comprehensive funnels that guide your audience through each stage of their journey.

Mailchimp, although primarily known for email marketing, it also offers powerful automation features. Use Mailchimp to set up automated email sequences that nurture leads based on their behavior and engagement with your content.

Canva is a versatile design tool that can help you create visually appealing landing pages. Use Canva's templates to design professional graphics and layouts that align with your brand identity.

Fiverr is an online marketplace that connects freelancers with clients who need various services. It operates on a gig-based system by which freelancers list their services at set prices, and clients can browse and purchase these services. Fiverr covers a vast array of categories, making it a versatile platform for both freelancers and clients. The platform is known for its accessibility and the broad range of services offered at competitive prices.

Hoppy Copy is a digital tool designed to streamline the process of creating marketing copy using AI technology. It's particularly focused on email marketing, but also supports the creation of various types of content. Hoppy Copy aims to save time and effort for marketers, entrepreneurs, and businesses by providing easy-to-use templates and customization options, ensuring that the generated content is engaging and effective.

LeadPages is a powerful tool for building landing pages. It offers a range of customizable templates optimized for conversions, allowing you to create effective landing pages without any coding knowledge.

Social Connector is a service designed to streamline and enhance the process of integrating various social media platforms and channels. It allows businesses to manage and connect their social media accounts all in one place so that there is better coordination, content distribution, and engagement tracking. It also allows for automation capabilities, including auto-replies, scheduled posts, and content creation.

ManyChat is a powerful chatbot platform designed for Facebook Messenger and other messaging apps. Removing the need for constant human intervention, this enables businesses to create automated chatbots that can engage with customers, provide information, and drive sales.

Bombbomb.com is a versatile tool for enhancing your email communications, specifically with the power of video.

Metricool is a comprehensive digital marketing tool that offers a range of services designed to help businesses and marketers analyze, manage, and optimize their online presence. It's best known for its detailed analytics, social media management, content scheduling, competitor analysis, and team collaboration tools. Its interface is intuitive and makes it possible for users of all skill levels to navigate its features easily.

As you consider the type of business you're building, you may need to use four or more different services to support your goal. Technology advances regularly, so invest the time to understand what is available to you that best addresses your needs. These services do come at a subscription cost, and usually offer a savings if you pay annually.

SOCIAL CAPITAL HIGHLIGHTS

- **Build and Own Your Email Distribution List.** An email distribution list is a valuable asset that you own, unlike social media profiles that can be hacked or locked. Use it for promotions, nurturing relationships, launching new products, and increasing return business.

- **Create Compelling Landing Pages.** A landing page focuses on converting visitors into leads or customers by using clear headlines, focused content, high-quality visuals, and strong calls to action (CTAs). It's a cost-effective way to drive conversions compared to a full website.

- **Leverage Funnels and Automation.** Funnels guide potential customers through a journey from awareness to action, while automation tools like FloDesk, ClickFunnels, and Mailchimp streamline email sequences and marketing tasks, enhancing efficiency and engagement.

- **Utilize Design and Analytical Tools.** Tools like Canva and LeadPages help create professional graphics and optimized landing pages, while Google Analytics and Metricool provide detailed insights into user behavior and marketing performance, allowing for continuous improvement.

- **Integrate Social Media and Messaging Platforms.** Services like Social Connector streamline social media management, and ManyChat automates customer engagement through chatbots, enhancing your ability to connect with and support customers across multiple channels.

Chapter 14

WORRIER OR WARRIOR

In the journey of launching and growing your own business, you have a crucial choice to make: Will you be a worrier or a warrior?

The worrier frets over every bump in the road, allowing stress and anxiety to hijack her dreams. This path leads to sleepless nights and a constant feeling of being overwhelmed. The weight of this choice impacts your life. Worrying can paralyze you, keeping you stuck in a cycle of doubt and inaction. It's important to be prepared and ready to break free from the chains of worry and choose a different path—one of empowerment and action.

Embrace the warrior mentality! Warriors do not back down from a challenge. They see obstacles as opportunities to grow and improve. They thrive on the thrill of the unknown, ready to improvise and adapt as situations arise. When warriors encounter a setback, they don't crumble—they rise, stronger and more determined than before. They adopt the pivot mentality—a willingness to learn and change course based on their new information. This mindset doesn't just lead to breakthroughs, it transforms every struggle into a steppingstone toward success.

The power behind this is your mental strength and preparedness.

Knowing your game plan *before* you hit a crisis or setback is what can improve the steps you take.

When my daughter was going through her developmental years (age two to four), she required a lot of redirections and corrections to her behavior. Her natural reaction was anger, frustration, and sassiness. She thought the world revolved around her, and she was going to get what she wanted. My hope, as her mother, was to raise a thoughtful, kind, and hard-working young lady. She required my full attention to make that happen. At the time, I was in a mother's Bible Study, surrounded by mothers with children of all ages. I learned so much from them.

They taught me the power and importance of knowing how we would handle her tantrums before they even occurred. By preparing for them, we didn't need to react or fall victim to being frustrated ourselves when they happened. Rather, we recognized that she needed us to help teach her and guide her. She didn't need her parents to react with frustration.

We implemented our strategy with collectiveness and a clear head. It was wonderful because we were able to teach her instead of trying to manage her. The lesson taught us how powerful it is to pre-determine our approach and reaction to a situation before it's in front of us.

Adopting a warrior spirit in business means taking control of your narrative. It's about harnessing your inner strength and believing in your ability to overcome any obstacle before it's ever in front of you. It's a far superior idea, compared to letting fear dictate your actions. Like in the game of chess, you channel that energy into bold, decisive moves, often thinking several steps ahead of your current move.

If you're going to write your own story, why not make it a bestseller? Make yourself the hero of your own story. Every challenge you conquer adds to your legacy of resilience and triumph.

Warrior Spirit in Modern-Day Business

One well-known story that shows how important the warrior spirit is in business is the turnaround of Apple Inc. under the leadership of Steve Jobs.

In 1997, Apple was struggling. The company was on the brink of bankruptcy, with declining sales and a series of failed products. Steve Jobs, who had co-founded Apple but was ousted in 1985, returned to the company when Apple acquired his startup, NeXT. His return marked the beginning of one of the most dramatic business turnarounds in history.

Acting with a Warrior Spirit

Vision and Innovation

Jobs immediately set to work, focusing on simplifying Apple's product line and concentrating on innovation. He understood that Apple needed a clear vision and began developing groundbreaking products. This led to the creation of the iMac, iPod, iPhone, and iPad—devices that would revolutionize the tech industry and consumer electronics.

Resilience and Determination

Jobs faced significant challenges, including internal resistance and external skepticism. However, he maintained a warrior mentality, believing in his vision and pushing forward despite the odds. His resilience was evident in how he navigated the complexities of redesigning Apple's product strategy and revitalizing the brand.

Strategic Decisions and Adaptation

One of Jobs' key moves was forging a partnership with Microsoft, which included an investment and a commitment to develop software for the Mac. This controversial decision provided much-needed capital and validated Apple's platform. Jobs also embraced new business models, such as opening retail stores and launching the iTunes Store, adapting to the changing digital landscape.

The Result

Through Jobs' warrior-like determination and innovative mindset, Apple went from near bankruptcy to becoming one of the most valuable companies in the world. The products developed under his leadership not only saved the company but also set new standards in technology and design, influencing countless industries. Chances are, you have owned several products that are a result of his innovation.

Steve Jobs' story with Apple illustrates the power of a warrior spirit in business. By maintaining a clear vision, showing resilience in the face of challenges, and making strategic, bold decisions, Jobs transformed Apple from a failing company into a global leader in innovation.

An Empowering Word

There's never been a time such as this. You have lived through and endured so much that the battle scars you have are a testament to your courage, grit, and fortitude. If there is an idea inside of you bursting with creative energy and you have a willingness to pursue it, why wait?

Fear of failure? That's not what stings. Regret is the real kicker. Embrace optimism and strength, and you'll find the entrepreneurial journey exhilarating. Sure, keeping momentum can be tough, especially when obstacles pop up. But remember, confidence is born from action, and resilience from repeated effort.

Start by tackling each step one at a time. Embrace your warrior spirit and armor up with determination. You'll be amazed at how innovative, strong, and incredible you truly are! This is a special time in your life, and change is thrilling. If you're ready to start your business, there's no better time than now. Let's make it happen!

SOCIAL CAPITAL HIGHLIGHTS

- **Choose Empowerment Over Worry:** Break free from the chains of worry and embrace a warrior mentality. Worrying leads to stress and paralysis, while a warrior's mindset empowers you to take action, face challenges, and grow stronger.
- **Prepare and Adapt:** Like a warrior ready for battle, be prepared to pivot and adapt to new information and challenges. Knowing your game plan before a crisis hits

enables you to respond with clarity and strength, turning obstacles into opportunities.

- **Control Your Narrative:** Harness your inner strength and believe in your ability to overcome any obstacle. Take control of your story, make bold decisions, and turn every challenge into a testament to your resilience and triumph.

GRATITUDE

*G*od, Thank You for Your mercy and favor and for Your eternal promises for our future and protection.

Ryan, you have always been my biggest supporter. With every crazy, outlandish, and exceptional idea, you have always maintained calm. Your willingness to support, invest, love, and help me is what I always dreamt of finding in life. You are my best friend and most loyal supporter. I love the life we have built and look forward to every adventure we have ahead of us. Thank you for making our life beautiful and full of love, laughter, and adventure.

Ellorie, you are my heart beating outside of my body. You are beautifully and wonderfully made. You are the light of our lives, and God made you perfectly. You are our greatest adventure. I pray you see that with all things in life, if you work for it, you can make anything happen. With God leading the way, friends around you who support you, and a family who loves you, the greatest riches are already yours. As I look at you, growing in faith, spirit, knowledge, and hope, I want you to know that when it comes to you, I am well pleased.

Mom and Dad, many years ago you made decisions that have impacted my life in great ways. Thank you for sitting outside of my piano lessons, Mom. The years of service playing for mass, celebrations, weddings, and funerals have surely touched many lives. Thank you, Dad for driving me for twelve weeks straight to Dale Carnegie Training when I was in middle school. So much impact occurred because you were willing to invest that time in me. I will always remember our time together on the car rides there and back. Mom and Dad, I know you both aimed to give us better opportunities than you had yourselves. Thank you for giving me skillsets, a worldly outlook, and the education needed to build this beautiful life. I do hope that you see with every decision, it was a set-up for a future that we could create for ourselves.

Maria, you are the first person I call when I can't figure something out. You have been on the receiving end of questions about everything. You've always been a safe person to come to. Thank you for your unwavering love.

Angela, you are the greatest teller of stories. The times in life I have belly laughed the most is when you are with me. You are strong, resilient, and a true example of the kind of person we should all aspire to be.

Britney Kensmoe, your friendship makes me a better person. My car-karaoke partner, 90's rap-master, personal hype-girl. You have always met me where I am. You've given me thoughtful ideas to consider and pushed me to always be in the best position possible. You've said my name in rooms I wasn't in. You've made it possible to meet people whose relationships you established years prior. Your trust and love mean everything to me. I thank you for your support through this exciting process.

Katie Keogh, your support, encouragement, and never-ending love have filled my life with such joy. We love adventuring with you and your family and feel so lucky that we both moved to North Carolina together. The bonds we have are deep, and the parallels of our lives always continue to surprise me. I love that we can laugh together, grow, and share life's beautiful moments.

Suzel Roth, you always have a way with the lens of a camera. Thank you for capturing me in my spirited ways so that it would translate through the images of my brand. You were the very first person I met when we moved in Raleigh. You were the first to invite me to the Ladies Dining Out group. You epitomize the behaviors and willingness to bring people into your network by being intentional and thoughtful. Thank you for seeing me and being my friend.

Mindy McFeaters, my life is in motion because of you. You are the reason I feel confident in pursuing big dreams. I know that whatever issues or projects I envision, they can be entrusted to your hands. You always have an open mind when I come to you with an idea or problem. I adore you and think the way your mind works is extraordinary.

Diane Miller, you have such an incredible skillset in making people cultivate their space, it's astounding! I love shopping with you; your brain sees things in a way I can't detect. You're brilliant, kind, and a master hostess. I thank you for designing an office environment where I was motivated to write and teach from.

Mike and Judy Stevens, thank you for your wisdom and friendship. You were the very first to read this manuscript in its entirety. Your thorough review along with welcomed input and ideas made this book even better. I will cherish our time spent together comparing words and meanings to make sure the right choices were made. This book has a lot of your heart in it.

My Referral Partners, you are the testimony to the successful techniques and approaches within this book. With your partnership, we have been able to help a ton of people. Your friendship means so much to me. I care deeply about your success and feel so fortunate to work alongside you as we pursue our dreams together.

Gomer Girls Bible Study, it was one Wednesday night as we were talking when it hit me that maybe it was time for me to tackle new things in life. Your warm and safe environment allows us all to grow, and to discuss and expand our understanding of His plans for our future. I'm so grateful for you all.

My past, current, and future Social Capital Academy Clients, you encourage me to continue strengthening my own resolve and show up in ways that make an impact. You are the reason I show up online and the reason I look forward to teaching women how to elevate their business both online and in person.

Shanda Trofe, thank you for making the process of writing, editing, and publishing this work so smooth.

And to you, if you're reading this book and we were able to spend time together, I thank you for sharing this time together. Your business is such a personal endeavor, and your time is valuable. I think you're amazing and have so much respect for you. Keep building your empire, girl. You've got this!

ABOUT THE AUTHOR

Katrina Wagner is a spirited entrepreneur, dedicated wife, and mom to Ellorie and two adorable fur babies, Charlie the Maltese and Dolly the Bichapoo. She grew up in Capac, Michigan on a forty-acre farm with her two sisters Maria and Angela. Their childhood was filled with the outdoors, animals, and wide-open spaces.

They hosted international exchange students for thirteen years. Katrina has had the chance to travel much of the world visiting her family. She spent six weeks in Hamamatsu, Japan as an exchange student the summer after she graduated from high school. Her love of travel was accentuated with time spent studying abroad during her senior year in college.

As someone who makes the most of the time she's given, Katrina triple-majored in International Business, Business Management, and Advertising at Northwood University. She was the student body president as a junior (a role usually reserved for seniors) and credits her time there to discovering the power of vision, purpose, and the art of connecting with people.

Fresh out of college, she started her first business, Dynamisis, LLC, offering internal operations consulting to family-run businesses in Metro-Detroit. But life had more exciting plans in store!

She found love in the digital age, meeting her amazing husband Ryan on e-Harmony.com. Together, they opened an insurance agency in Livonia, Michigan two weeks after they were married. Then, they welcomed their daughter Ellorie into their lives in 2014. Fast forward to 2019, they made a bold move to North Carolina, embracing the thrill of new beginnings. They moved to build a life they loved.

As the pandemic unfolded, Katrina launched her own insurance agency in Raleigh, NC. In just four years, she built a thriving business with delighted customers and a vibrant network of referral partners. After successfully selling the agency, she is now on a mission to empower others to transform their dreams into reality.

Katrina is a sushi lover, travel enthusiast, and local boutique shopper. Connect with her on Instagram @ TheKatrinaWagner and @ KatrinaWagner.BusinessBFF. Find her on Facebook: The Katrina Wagner. Dive into the resources section for free tools and insights tailored for today's modern entrepreneur. There you will also be able to access her top-rated course, Social Capital Academy.

SOCIAL CAPITAL ACADEMY

www.TheKatrinaWagner.com
www.TheSocialCapitalAcademy.com

www.ingramcontent.com/pod-product-compliance
Lightning Source LLC
Chambersburg PA
CBHW071422210326
41597CB00020B/3615